endorsed for
Edexcel

T0351609

Edexcel GCSE (9-1)
Religious Studies B

Paper 2: Religion, Peace and Conflict: Islam

Series Editor: Lynne Gibson   Author: Tanya Hill

Pearson

Published by Pearson Education Limited, 80 Strand, London, WC2R 0RL.

www.pearsonschoolsandfecolleges.co.uk

Copies of official specifications for all Edexcel qualifications may be found on the website: www.edexcel.com

Text © Pearson Education Limited 2016
Series editor: Lynne Gibson
Typeset by Tek-Art
Produced by Hart Mcleod Ltd
Cover design by Malena Wilson-Max
Picture research by Sarah Hopper
Cover photo/illustration © Connie Coleman / Ocean / Corbis

The right of Tanya Hill to be identified as author of this work has been asserted by her in accordance with the Copyright, Designs and Patents Act 1988.

First published 2016

24

10 9 8 7 6

British Library Cataloguing in Publication Data

A catalogue record for this book is available from the British Library

ISBN 978 1 292 1396 4

Copyright notice

All rights reserved. No part of this publication may be reproduced in any form or by any means (including photocopying or storing it in any medium by electronic means and whether or not transiently or incidentally to some other use of this publication) without the written permission of the copyright owner, except in accordance with the provisions of the Copyright, Designs and Patents Act 1988 or under the terms of a licence issued by the Copyright Licensing Agency, Barnards Inn, 86 Fetter Lane, London EC4A 1EN (www.cla.co.uk). Applications for the copyright owner's written permission should be addressed to the publisher.

Printed by Ashford Colour Press Ltd

Acknowledgements

The author and publisher would like to thank the following individuals and organisations for permission to reproduce photographs:

Alamy Images: Art Directors & TRIP 55l, Mohammed Anwarul Kabir Choudhury 16, epa european pressphoto agency b.v. 61, 112, Granger, NYC 117, Images & Stories 55r, National Geographic Creative 27, Radius Images 67-68, Mahmoud Rahall 79, Marco Secchi 21, Visuals Stock 37-38, World Religions Photo Library 42; **Bridgeman Art Library Ltd:** Pictures from History 114, © PVDE 24; **Fotolia.com:** a4stockphotos 69, ArenaCreative 31, elmirex2009 57, kesipun 97-98, Prazis 7-8, Seamartini Graphics 49; **Getty Images:** AFP 109, Yousef Albalawi 19, Dimas Ardian 99, Photofusion 121, Mohamed El-Shahed 60r, STR / AFP 78, Zerbor 95; **Courtesy of Mosaic:** 73; **Reuters:** Bazuki Muhammad 66; **Courtesy of Salaam Peace:** 103b; **Shutterstock.com:** G. Campbell 72, dolphfyn 84, Sinan Isakovic 35, Lou Oates 90; **TopFoto:** Ann Ronan Picture Library / Heritage Images 30, Fine Art Images / HIP 87; **The Walters Art Museum, Baltimore:** 75

Cover images: *Front:* **Corbis:** 2 / Connie Coleman / Ocean

All other images © Pearson Education

Text

The author and publisher would like to thank The Islamic Foundation/Kube Publishing and Darussalam International for permission to reproduce the following text extracts:

All Qur'anic quotations from *The Meaning of the Holy Qur'an* 3rd ed., The Islamic Foundation/Kube Publishing (Abdullah Yusuf Ali 2009); Extract on page 126 from *Al Muwatta of Imam Malik*, Darussalam International (Imam Malik); Extracts on pages 11, 16 and 91 from *Hadith: Sahih Muslim*, Darussalam International (translated by Nasiruddin Al-Khattab); Extract on page 28 from *Hadith: Sahih Al-Bukhari, Volume 8*, Darussalam International.

Websites

Pearson Education Limited is not responsible for the content of any external internet sites. It is essential for tutors to preview each website before using it in class so as to ensure that the URL is still accurate, relevant and appropriate. We suggest that tutors bookmark useful websites and consider enabling students to access them through the school/college intranet.

A note from the publisher

In order to ensure that this resource offers high-quality support for the associated Pearson qualification, it has been through a review process by the awarding body. This process confirms that this resource fully covers the teaching and learning content of the specification or part of a specification at which it is aimed. It also confirms that it demonstrates an appropriate balance between the development of subject skills, knowledge and understanding, in addition to preparation for assessment.

Endorsement does not cover any guidance on assessment activities or processes (e.g. practice questions or advice on how to answer assessment questions), included in the resource nor does it prescribe any particular approach to the teaching or delivery of a related course.

While the publishers have made every attempt to ensure that advice on the qualification and its assessment is accurate, the official specification and associated assessment guidance materials are the only authoritative source of information and should always be referred to for definitive guidance.

Pearson examiners have not contributed to any sections in this resource relevant to examination papers for which they have responsibility.

Examiners will not use endorsed resources as a source of material for any assessment set by Pearson.

Endorsement of a resource does not mean that the resource is required to achieve this Pearson qualification, nor does it mean that it is the only suitable material available to support the qualification, and any resource lists produced by the awarding body shall include this and other appropriate resources.

Contents

How to use this book

What's covered?

This book covers Islam: Religion, peace and ethics. This area of study makes up 50% of your GCSE course and will be examined in Paper 2.

This area of study focuses on the teachings, beliefs and practices of Islam. You need to understand these aspects of the religion within British society today. This book also explains the different types of exam questions you will need to answer, and includes advice and example answers to help you improve.

Features

As well as a clear, detailed explanation of the key knowledge you will need, you will also find a number of features in the book:

Specialised terminology and Glossary

All the key words and terms are written in bold for easy reference. Explanations of what they all mean are given in the glossary at the back of the book.

Activities

Every few pages, you'll find a box containing some activities designed to help you check and embed knowledge and get you to really think about what you've studied. The activities start simple, but might get more challenging as you work through them.

Can you remember?

Throughout the chapter, these features ask you to recall facts from previous topics to reinforce your learning. These features encourage you to draw links between different beliefs and understand how they are incorporated into people's lives today. This will help you to remember the information and be able to access it again later. Revisit these as part of your revision, too.

> **Can you remember?**
>
> - How do the pillars of Sawm and Hajj relate to the festivals of Id-ul-Adha and Id-ul-Fitr?
> - Why is it important to Muslims to recognise the history of Islam?
> - Why do Muslims believe the prophets are so important in Islam?

Sources of authority

Throughout the topics you'll find quotations from sources of wisdom and authority such as the Qur'an and the Bible. They are highlighted in separate boxes so you can find them easily and use them as a revision tool.

> **Sources of authority**
>
> *The adhan*
> *Allah is the Greatest (say three times)*
> *I bear witness that there is no god but Allah (say twice)*
> *I bear witness that Muhammad is Allah's messenger (say twice)*
> *Rush to prayer (say twice)*
> *Rush to success (say twice)*
> *Allah is the Greatest (say twice)*
> *There is no god but Allah.*

Extend your knowledge

At the end of each section, you'll find a box containing additional information that will help you gain a deeper understanding of the topic. This could be an alternative interpretation, a short biography of an important person or extra background information about an event. Information in these boxes is not essential to your exam success, but will provide you with valuable insights.

Exam-style questions and tips

This book also includes extra exam-style questions you can use to practise. These appear in the chapters and are accompanied by a tip to help you get started on an answer.

> **Exam-style questions**
>
> Explain two reasons why prophets are so important in Islam. (4 marks)

> **Exam tip**
>
> Make sure you give two different reasons to answer this question. For each reason, explain your ideas fully, giving examples to show what you mean.

Summaries and Checkpoints

At the end of each topic, the main points are summarised in a series of bullet points – great for embedding the core knowledge, and handy for revision.

Checkpoints help you to check and reflect on your learning: The Strengthen section helps you to consolidate your knowledge and understanding, and check that you've grasped the basic ideas and concepts. The Challenge questions push you to go beyond just understanding the information, and into evaluation and analysis of what you've studied.

Recap

At the end of each chapter, you'll find the Recap section, designed to help you consolidate and reflect on the chapter as a whole. Each Recap spread includes a recall quiz, ideal for quickly checking your knowledge or for revision. They also include activities designed to help you summarise and analyse what you've learned, and also reflect on how each chapter links to other parts of the unit.

Recap quiz

The Six Beliefs of Islam

1 Name each of the Six Beliefs of Islam for Sunni Muslims.
2 How are the Six Beliefs of Islam for Sunni Muslims put into practice in everyday life?

The Five Roots of 'Usul ad-Din in Shi'a Islam

3 Name each of the Five Roots of 'Usul ad-Din for Shi'a Muslims.
4 How are the Five Roots of 'Usul ad-Din for Shi'a Muslims put into practice in everyday life?
5 What are the key differences between Sunni and Shi'a Muslims?

The nature of Allah

6 State five characteristics of Allah.
7 Name five of the 99 names of Allah.
8 How are beliefs about Allah seen to be central to the religion of Islam?

Extend

At the end of each chapter, there is an opportunity to read and work with a piece of text related to the chapter's learning. It might be an anecdote or description of an event, a personal viewpoint or an opportunity to look at more sacred texts. Tasks based on the passage will help you apply your knowledge to new contexts and bring together aspects of your learning from across the course.

Extend: Muslim beliefs

Source

Hello, my name is Rayan. I am a Muslim and this means I follow the religion of Islam. I will tell you a little bit about my faith. I believe in one God and call him Allah. I pray to him five times every day – sometimes with my family and sometimes alone. I also try to attend the Mosque on a Friday.

My family and I belong to the largest branch of Islam – it is known as Sunni Islam. We believe in life after death, and that the prophets are Allah's way of communicating with us, and we believe what the holy books tell us. I read the Islamic holy book, the Qur'an, every day. It makes me feel closer to Allah and understand him better.

Preparing for your exams

At the back of the book, you'll find a special section dedicated to explaining and exemplifying the new Edexcel GCSE Religious Studies exams. Each question type is explained through annotated sample answers at two levels, showing clearly how answers can be improved. There are also plenty of practice questions, with more tips to get you started.

1 Muslim beliefs

Islam is estimated to be the second largest religion, representing approximately 20 per cent of the world's population. It is also the fastest growing. It originated in Saudi Arabia in the 7th century CE. The word 'Islam' means 'voluntary submission to God', and followers are called Muslims, which means 'someone who surrenders themselves to the will of God'. It is a **monotheistic** religion, accepting belief in one God, who Muslims call **Allah**. Muslims follow the teachings of the **Prophet Muhammad**, their prophet. He was born in **Makkah** in 570 CE and was a messenger of Allah, who brought the Qur'an, the Islamic holy book.

There are two main branches, or denominations, within Islam: the **Sunnis** and the **Shi'as**. Sunni Islam represents approximately 90 per cent of the world's Muslims, and Shi'a Islam about 10 per cent. While the two groups share many beliefs and practices, they differ in their ideas on leadership, their interpretation of the Qur'an and some ritual practices.

A third group is **Sufism**. This is a small group of Muslims who believe it is important to learn about Islam from teachers rather than holy books. Sufis have helped to shape Islamic thought.

Learning objectives

In this chapter you will find out about:

- the Six Beliefs of Islam
- the Five Roots of 'Usul ad-Din in Shi'a Islam
- the nature of Allah
- Risalah (prophethood)
- Muslim holy books
- Malaikah (angels)
- al-Qadr (predestination)
- Akhirah (life after death).

Checkpoint

Recall

Before starting this chapter, you should remember:

- Islam is a major world religion, which is continuing to grow
- there are two main branches in Islam – Sunni Islam and Shi'a Islam
- different Muslims may practise and interpret their faith differently
- all Muslims are united by shared beliefs, such as the acceptance of Muhammad as the final prophet, the Qur'an as their holy book and the importance of Islam being a 'way of life'.

Look ahead

In future chapters you will find out about:

- what it means to live a Muslim life
- Islamic beliefs and attitudes towards crime and punishment
- Islamic beliefs and attitudes towards peace and conflict.

1.1 The Six Beliefs of Islam

- To understand the nature, history and purpose of the Six Beliefs of Islam, including the Kitab al-iman.
- To recognise the importance of these principles for Muslims.
- To explore how they are understood and expressed in Sunni and Shi'a Muslim communities today.

The Six Beliefs

The Six Beliefs of Islam are the basic beliefs that Sunni Muslim holds to be true. They are:

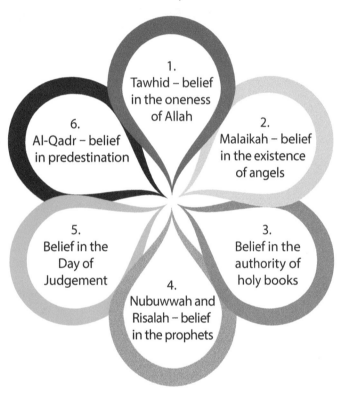

Figure 1.1 The Six Beliefs of Islam that every Sunni Muslim accepts

1. Tawhid – belief in the oneness of Allah

This is a central belief in Islam. Islam is a monotheistic faith, meaning Muslims accept that there is only one God. Muslims call their God Allah and believe that part of being a Muslim is to carry out Allah's will, to submit or surrender themselves to him.

2. Malaikah – belief in the existence of angels

Muslims accept the existence of angels. Angels are believed to be created from light and have no physical bodies, although they do have the ability to take on human form. Islam teaches that Malaikah have no free will, which means that they cannot make their own choices. Instead they are completely obedient to Allah's commands. They are important to Muslims as it is through them that Allah is believed to have communicated messages to his **prophets**, or messengers, who in turn share them with human beings.

3. Belief in the authority of holy books

The name of the Islamic holy book is the **Qur'an**. It is believed to be the final perfect message received from Allah by the Prophet Muhammad. Islam is centred around these teachings. Muslims also recognise the importance of other holy books shared with the other **Abrahamic** religions of Judaism and Christianity. These include the scrolls of Abraham, the scrolls of Moses, the Torah, the Psalms and the Gospel. This is because Islam is an Abrahamic faith, meaning that it traces its roots back to the Prophet Abraham.

4. Nubuwwah and Risalah – belief in the prophets

Muslims believe that one of the ways Allah communicates with human beings is through prophets. A prophet is a messenger from Allah and the link between Allah and humans. Messages are usually communicated to the prophets through Malaikah. The prophets' messages are considered to be the word of Allah and are recorded in the holy books. **Nubuwwah** is the Islamic term for prophethood. The Islamic word **Risalah** literally refers to the communication link or channel between Allah and humans. Prophets recognised in Islam include Nuh (Noah), Ibrahim (Abraham), Musa (Moses), Isa (Jesus) and Muhammad, the most important, who is considered the founder of Islam. As a sign of respect to Muhammad, Muslims say 'peace be upon him' after his name.

5. Belief in the Day of Judgement

Muslims believe in the afterlife and that after death they will have to account for their actions. They accept that there will be a **Day of Judgement** when the whole world ends. The Day of Judgement is a day in the future where every human that has ever existed will be judged by Allah on their actions in their life on Earth. Allah will decide who should be rewarded with a place in **al-Jannah**, Paradise, and who should be punished in **Jahannam,** or Hell. The belief in the Day of Judgement is important to all Muslims because it directs their behaviour in their lives on Earth, knowing that their future life is dependent on this.

6. Al-Qadr – belief in predestination

Predestination is the idea that Allah knows everything, and Sunni Muslims believe that although human beings have free will to make their own choices, Allah anticipates and knows what will happen. Sunni Muslims believe that they need to trust Allah to know what is best for them. Although this idea appears to contradict that of the idea of humans having free will, it does not mean that Allah influences their decisions, only that he is aware of the decisions every human will make before they are made. Shi'a Muslims do not accept the belief of predestination.

The Six Beliefs of Islam are found in the **Kitab al-iman**, 'The Book of Faith'. This is a book that brings together these key beliefs and focuses on them, explaining the Six Beliefs of Islam for Sunni Muslims in detail. It was written in the 13th century by an Islamic scholar called Ibn Taymiyyah and acts as a guide to the practice of holding these key beliefs.

What is the purpose of the Six Beliefs of Islam?

The Six Beliefs of Islam are seen to:

- unite all Sunni Muslims as they share them in common; they show what it means to be a Muslim and help Sunni Muslims all over the world feel part of the Muslim community, or **ummah**
- help Sunni Muslims to understand their religion better; they identify the key ideas and beliefs of the religion, highlighting the importance of those things that are important, which might direct their behaviour in life. For example, Sunni Muslim beliefs about Allah and the Day of Judgement encourage them to be more aware of how they treat others and how they follow the rules of Islam within their lives as they believe that after death, Allah will judge them on the Day of Judgement to determine their reward or punishment
- support Sunni Muslims in directing how they should live, as the Six Beliefs will impact on their actions and behaviour. The Six Beliefs guide them to understand what Allah wants and how they should try to act within the world.

How important are the Six Beliefs of Islam for Muslims?

The Six Beliefs of Islam are the fundamental beliefs that every Sunni Muslim must accept in order to be considered a Muslim. The most important of these beliefs is Tawhid, a belief in the oneness of Allah. This is at the centre of Muslim faith and connects all other beliefs.

Although the Six Beliefs of Islam are recognised in this way by Sunni Muslims, Shi'a Muslims recognise the ideas but understand and express them differently. They instead have the five roots of 'Usul ad-Din which hold many similarities to the Six Beliefs. These will be explained in further detail in the next chapter.

How are the Six Beliefs of Islam understood and expressed in Sunni Muslim communities today?

Islam affects every aspect of the life of a Muslim, so the Six Beliefs of Islam are daily considerations for every Muslim. Muslims are always aware of their key beliefs, and try to live according to them.

- Muslims think about the belief in Tawhid, the oneness of God, every day. It is stated in the **Shahadah**, Declaration of Faith, and forms part of their prayers, which happen five times a day.
- Muslims turn to holy books, especially the Qur'an, for advice on what they should believe about issues such as the nature of Allah and **resurrection**. Holy books contain the messages of the prophets, as well as other essential beliefs about predestination, Malaikah and the Day of Judgement.
- Muslims try to follow the example of the Prophet Muhammad in the way they live. They look to his example of how they should behave. They also refer to the **Hadith**, which is another Holy Book that contains accounts of reports about Muhammad.
- Muslims live their lives believing that after death, Allah will judge them on their actions. If they live as Allah wants them to, they believe they will be rewarded with paradise in the afterlife. If they do not live as Allah wants, Muslims believe they will be eternally punished in hell.
- Muslims try to be aware of every action they perform in their lives. They are constantly aware that their behaviour will determine their afterlife and they consider whether their actions are what Allah would wish them to do. Their religion and beliefs cause them to consider the way they live according to the laws of Allah.

Activities

1. Explain what your top six beliefs are. Think of an example for each one to illustrate how you express your beliefs in your daily life.

2. Create your own summary diagram of the Six Beliefs of Islam, making sure you explain what each one is and why it is important in your own words.

3. Get into groups of six and give each person in your group one of the beliefs to concentrate on. Make sure you learn the information about your belief thoroughly, as you are your group's 'expert'. Complete a 'hot seat' activity where members of your group ask you questions about your belief.

Exam tip

The exam requires you to outline three different ways in which Sunni Muslims demonstrate their belief in the Six Beliefs. Be specific in your answer to demonstrate your knowledge to the examiner.

Exam-style questions

Outline three ways the Six beliefs of Islam are expressed for Sunni Muslims today. **(3 marks)**

Sources of authority

Abu Huraira reported: 'One day the Messenger of Allah (may peace be upon him) appeared before the public that a man came to him and said: "Prophet of Allah [tell me] what is Iman?" Upon this he (the Holy Prophet) replied: "That you affirm your faith in Allah, His angels, His books, His meeting, His Messengers and that you affirm your faith in the Resurrection hereafter."' (Kitab al-iman 1:4)

Extend your knowledge

'Iman' is the Arabic word for 'faith' or 'belief'. It is the term used for belief in the Six Beliefs of Islam. Care should be taken with this term, as it does not mean 'blind belief' but more the idea of faith through reason, where Muslims accept the key ideas because they make sense rationally.

Summary

- The Six Beliefs of Islam are the key beliefs held by every Sunni Muslim. They are:
  - Tawhid – the oneness of Allah
  - the existence of Malaikah, or angels
  - the authority of holy books
  - prophethood
  - the Day of Judgement
  - predestination.
- Sunni Muslims express their acceptance of these beliefs in different ways. The beliefs are considered to be important and affect the way Sunni Muslims live and behave.

Checkpoint

Strengthen

S1 Can you name the Six Beliefs of Islam and explain each one?

S2 How could Sunni Muslims express the Six Beliefs of Islam in their lives today?

S3 How do the quotes in the Sources of authority box show the importance of the Six Beliefs of Islam?

Challenge

C1 In your own words, summarise two reasons why the Six Beliefs of Islam are essential to Sunni Muslims.

C2 Why might some Muslims argue that all of the Six Beliefs of Islam are equally important, while others feel that Tawhid is most important?

C3 Do you think it is more important for Sunni Muslims to express the Six Beliefs of Islam privately or publicly? Why?

1.2 The Five Roots of 'Usul ad-Din in Shi'a Islam

Learning objectives

- To understand the nature, history and purpose of the Five Roots of 'Usul ad-Din in Shi'a Islam.
- To identify the importance of these principles for different Shi'a communities today.

The Five Roots of 'Usul ad-Din

All Muslims accept the same basic beliefs within Islam. However, one key difference between Sunni and Shi'a Muslims is their understanding of the beliefs.

All Sunni Muslims accept the Six Beliefs of Islam. In contrast, Shi'a Muslims accept similar ideas but refer to them as the Five Roots of 'Usul ad-Din. This translates literally as 'foundation of faith', showing that they are the essential beliefs that all Shi'a Muslims accept.

The Five Roots of 'Usul ad-Din in Shi'a Islam are:

1. Tawhid – the oneness of God

All Muslims accept the idea that there is one God, known as Tawhid or monotheism. Shi'a Muslims believe the Qur'an is clear on Tawhid, stating in the Qur'an, Surah 112 that Allah is the one and only God who has no peers, no match and no partners. He is believed to be eternal, the first and the last.

2. 'Adl – justice and fairness

Shi'a Muslims believe that there is good and bad in everything. They believe that Allah commands human beings to do good things and avoid bad things. They accept that Allah acts in a just and fair way at all times to ensure equality. This idea is also held by Sunni Muslims, although it is not formally part of their belief system.

3. Nubuwwah – prophethood

As in Sunni Islam, Shi'a Muslims believe that Allah has appointed prophets and messengers to teach his message to humanity. This message involves instruction on how to live a life of submission to Allah, behaving as he wants. This would include Shi'a Muslims accepting and believing in the Five Roots of 'Usul ad-Din. They believe Muhammad was Allah's final messenger and that he brought the complete message to humanity. Islam teaches that Allah often communicates to his prophets through Malaikah. Muslims call the channel of communication between Allah and humanity Risalah.

4. Imamah – successors to Muhammad

In Sunni Islam, an imam is a religious leader or teacher, for instance, someone who might lead prayers in the mosque. Most Shi'a Muslims, however, believe that there have been 12 imams specially appointed by Allah throughout history as leaders to lead and guide humanity. They believe that imams were chosen by Allah to continue to teach his message correctly and they accept that there is only ever a single imam at any one time.

Can you remember?

- Can you remember what the Six Beliefs of Islam are for Sunni Muslims?
- Can you explain each one?
- Can you compare them to the Five Roots of 'Usul ad-Din for Shi'a Muslims and consider which are similar and which are different?

Sources of authority

Say: "He is Allah, the One and Only; Allah the Eternal, Absolute; He begets not, nor is He begotten; And there is none like unto Him." (Surah 112:1–4)

Sources of authority

Say you: "We believe in Allah, and the revelation given to us, and to Abraham, Ismail, Isaac, Jacob, and the Tribes, and that given to Moses and Jesus, and that given to (all) prophets from their Lord: we make no difference between one and another of them: and we bow to Allah (in Islam)." (Surah 2:136)

The last of these imams is believed to be the final prophet, Muhammad, which is why Muslims believe that his message should not be altered or changed in any way. Muslims accept that 11 of the imams were murdered before the next imam took their place, but they believe that the twelfth, Muhammad, is still alive but hidden by Allah. They believe that one day he will appear to bring an end to tyranny and oppression.

5. Mi'ad - The Day of Judgement and the Resurrection

Shi'a Muslims believe that one day in the future every human being that has ever existed will be brought back to life, or resurrected, before being judged by Allah. They believe the Qur'an makes it clear that there will be a resurrection of both soul and body and all humans will be judged on the way they acted and behaved within their lives. The acceptance of resurrection after death and the belief that there will be a Day of Resurrection is fundamental to all Muslims. It promotes the idea of a life after death and how Muslims live their lives now will affect whether Allah rewards or punishes them after their resurrection.

Why are the Five Roots of 'Usul ad-Din important to Shi'a communities today?

- They unite all Shi'a Muslims as an ummah, community, and form the basis of the religion. They show what it means to be a Muslim as they share these beliefs in common.
- They are often considered to be the foundations of the religion of Islam, holding it together. It helps to support the faith in establishing its key beliefs.
- They help Shi'a Muslims to understand their religion by identifying those beliefs that teach what they should accept and how they should behave. For example, accepting belief in Yawm al-Qiyyamah, the Day of Resurrection, means they consider every action they make as it will contribute towards this day when they will be judged.
- They help Shi'a Muslims understand their religion better and allow them to live as Allah intended. They guide Shi'a Muslims on understanding how Allah wants them to behave and act within the world.

Even though one branch of Islam is Shi'a Islam, within this, there are different groups of Muslims. Two of these

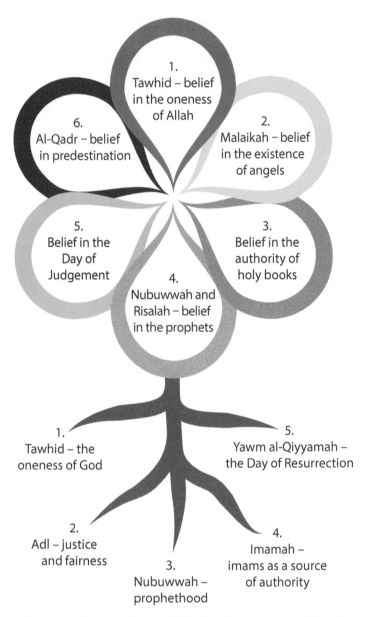

Figure 1.2 The Five Roots of 'Usul ad-Din are believed by all Shi'a Muslims

are known as the Seveners and Twelvers. Sevener Shi'a developed as they believe Isma'il Ibn Jafar was the seventh and last imam. The group known as the Twelvers are the largest Shi'a group, who accept there were twelve imams after the death of Muhammad. The five roots of 'Usul ad-Din are important to all Shi'a Muslims but especially for Sevener and Twelver communities as even though they may have slight differences, these serve to unite and hold them together. Also essential beliefs such as Imamah are contained in this, which is the basis of their beliefs in placing imams as a source of authority at the centre of their communities.

How do Sunni and Shi'a beliefs about the Five Roots of 'Usul ad-Din differ?

Sunni and Shi'a Muslims share many key beliefs in common, such as Tawhid, prophethood and the Day of Judgement and the Resurrection, as shown in Figure 1.2. Sunni Muslims accept that ideas of justice are important, but do not necessarily place the same emphasis on it as Shi'a Muslims. Shi'as recognise Adl as one of the five roots of 'Usul ad-Din. Sunni Muslims also do not place the same emphasis on the authority of imams. Sunnis believe they are important as a source of authority, but not specifically appointed by Allah as is the Shi'a understanding.

Activities

1   Write a magazine article for a Muslim magazine explaining the Five roots of 'Usul ad-Din for Muslim teenagers. Make sure you give enough detail to fully explain the importance of each idea.

2   Explain how Muslims may demonstrate their commitment to the Five roots of 'Usul ad-Din in their lives.

3   Which of the Five Roots of 'Usul ad-Din do you think is most important to a Muslim? Give two reasons for your answer. Share your ideas with other people to see if their answers are different.

Exam-style questions ○

Outline three reasons why the Five Roots of 'Usul ad-Din are important to Shi'a communities today.
(3 marks)

Exam tip ○

This question asks for three reasons, so make sure you outline three different ideas in your answer. Make sure you express them clearly.

Summary ◣

- Shi'a Muslims accept the Five Roots of 'Usul ad-Din. These are:
  - Tawhid, the oneness of Allah
  - Adl, that Allah is just and fair in all things
  - Nubuwwah or prophethood
  - Imamah, that imams are a source of authority
  - Yawm al-Qiyyamah, meaning the Day of Resurrection.
- These beliefs are important for Shi'a Muslim communities as they help to unite them and give them understanding of their faith.

Checkpoint ◣

Strengthen

S1 What are the main two branches of Muslims in Islam and which branch accepts the Five Roots of 'Usul ad-Din?

S2 Can you name the Five Roots of 'Usul ad-Din and explain each one?

S3 Why do you think Shi'a Muslims believe each of these beliefs is important?

Challenge

C1 Which belief do you think Shi'a Muslims consider to be the most important of the Five Roots of 'Usul ad-Din and why?

C2 How do you think the Five Roots of 'Usul ad-Din affect the life of a Shi'a Muslim?

C3 Why do you think Sunni and Shi'a Muslims hold slightly different beliefs?

1.3 The nature of Allah

Learning objectives

- To understand what Muslims believe about Allah.
- To consider how the characteristics of Allah are shown in the Qur'an.
- To explore why the characteristics of Allah are important to Muslims.

Sources of authority

The worshippers of false gods say: "If Allah had so willed, we should not have worshipped aught but Him—neither we nor our fathers,—nor should we have prescribed prohibitions other than His." So did those who went before them. But what is the mission of messengers but to preach the clear Message? For We assuredly sent amongst every people a messenger, (with the Command), "Serve Allah, and eschew Evil": of the people were some whom Allah guided, and some on whom error became inevitably (established). So travel through the earth, and see what was the end of those who denied (the Truth).

(Surah 16:35–36)

Sources of authority

And your Allah is One Allah. There is no god but He, Most Gracious, Most Merciful.
(Surah 2:163)

Islamic beliefs about Allah

Muslims believe there is only one God. They call him Allah, and they direct their worship and praise towards him. They believe that he is a supreme being with supernatural powers and that he is extremely special compared with human beings, so he must be shown the utmost respect. Muslims accept that Allah is the sole creator and designer of the world and everything in it. Moreover, they believe that Allah is also the sustainer of the universe, as he continues to rule and control everything.

Muslims also accept that Allah is transcendent. This means that he is above and beyond anything else that exists on Earth, and because of this the nature and actions of Allah are difficult for human beings to understand. Muslims use the word Tawhid to describe the idea that they believe in only one God. This is the most fundamental idea of Islam, accepted by all Muslims. They believe Allah has certain characteristics, which help them to understand what he is like.

Characteristic	Definition
Transcendent	He is above and beyond anything that exists in the world. This can make Allah difficult for Muslims to understand fully or describe.
Immanent	He is close to every human and acts within the world daily. Muslims believe that everything within the universe can point to Allah.
Omnipotent	He is all-powerful. This shows that Allah is in control of everything that happens and there is nothing more powerful than him.
Beneficent	He is all-loving and cares for his creations on a personal level.
Merciful	He forgives the things that people do wrong. He is compassionate when people are sorry.
Just	He judges people in a fair and unbiased way.

Shi'a Muslims also believe in **Adalat**, the idea that Allah is equitable and just. This term refers to how Shi'a Muslims believe Allah created the world in a just and fair way. Allah behaves in a fair and merciful manner at all times.

Allah and the Qur'an

A key Islamic belief for all Muslims is the oneness of Allah, or Tawhid. However, there are many different descriptions and therefore it can be difficult for Muslims to combine them into one clear understanding. Muslims also believe that Allah is transcendent and therefore cannot be described fully by words. The Qur'an teaches that Allah has 99 names, which are words or characteristics used to describe Allah. They help Muslims to think about the nature of Allah and make ideas about Allah easier to comprehend and relate to. Muslims may use a **subhah** when they pray, which is a set of 99 prayer beads to help them to remember and recite the 99 names. Muslims believe that being able to recall all 99 names of Allah strongly shows their devotion to him. This idea is reinforced in the Hadith: Abu Huraira reported the Prophet Muhammad as saying 'There are 99 names of Allah: he who commits them to memory will get into paradise.' (Hadith 35: 6475).

Figure 1.3 Muslims use subhah beads like these to help them in prayer when they are remembering the 99 names of Allah

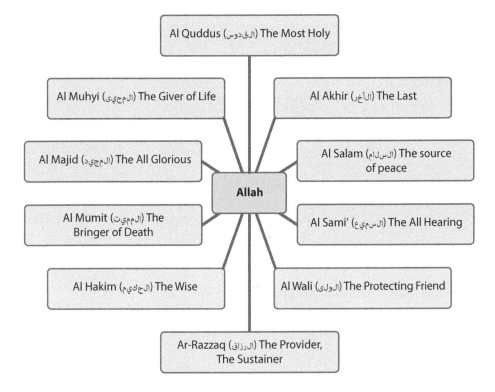

Al Quddus (القدوس) The Most Holy

Al Muhyi (المحيي) The Giver of Life

Al Akhir (الآخر) The Last

Al Majid (المجيد) The All Glorious

Al Salam (السلام) The source of peace

Allah

Al Mumit (المميت) The Bringer of Death

Al Sami' (السميع) The All Hearing

Al Hakim (الحكيم) The Wise

Al Wali (الولى) The Protecting Friend

Ar-Razzaq (الرزاق) The Provider, The Sustainer

Why are these characteristics important?

- They help Muslims to gain some understanding of the 'unknowable' nature of Allah. By having more understanding, Muslims can show Allah more respect, which they believe is an important part of being Muslim.
- They allow Muslims to get closer to Allah and develop a meaningful relationship with him.
- They are accepted by everyone in the worldwide Muslim ummah. This brings the ummah together and allows Muslims to talk about Allah and their shared beliefs in a meaningful way.
- They are contained in the Qur'an, which is the Islamic holy book revealed to Muhammad, so Muslims believe Allah wants them to know these characteristics.

Activities ?

1 Look at each of the words used to describe Allah and explain why you think these are suitable ways of explaining what he is like. As an extension, explain any other words you think they could use to describe what Allah is like.

2 Explain in your own words what Muslims believe about Allah.

3 Work in groups to discuss the idea of whether it is good to have names to describe Allah. Split your group equally, with one side agreeing that it is and the other disagreeing. Make sure you give reasons and examples for each argument you present. Once you have considered all the arguments, individually write down your own opinion.

Exam tip

Examiners require you to provide a reason and then develop it sufficiently in your explanation. You may want to include an example or relevant explanation of the relevance of prophets in the lives of Muslims.

Sources of authority

In the name of Allah, Most Gracious, Most Merciful,
Praise be to Allah, the Cherisher and Sustainer of the Worlds
Most Gracious, Most Merciful;
Master of the Day of Judgement,
You do we worship,
And Your aid we seek.
Show us the straight way.
The way of those on whom
You bestowed Your Grace,
Those whose (portion) is not wrath
And who go not astray. (Surah 1:1–7)

The most beautiful names belong to Allah: so call on him by them…
(Surah 7:180)

Exam-style questions

Explain two reasons why prophets are so important in Islam. **(4 marks)**

Summary

- Muslims believe Allah is unknowable and indescribable.
- Muslims give Allah characteristics to be able to talk about him and try to overcome the difficulties of not being able to know him.
- Muslims believe Allah is transcendent, immanent, omnipotent and beneficent.
- The key beliefs about the nature of Allah are contained in the Qur'an.
- Muslims use 99 names to describe the different characteristics of Allah.
- Muslims may use subhahs to help them remember the 99 names of Allah.

Checkpoint

Strengthen

S1 Where do Muslims get their beliefs about Allah from?

S2 Look at the passages in the Sacred Text box and use them to describe what Allah is like and what Allah is believed to be able to do.

S3 Why are the 99 names of Allah important for Muslims?

Challenge

C1 Why might some people feel that Allah's characteristics of transcendence and immanence contradict each other?

C2 What can you learn about Allah from the names he is given?

C3 Why might some people not accept Islamic ideas about God?

1.4 Risalah: prophethood

Learning objectives

- To understand the nature and importance of prophethood for Muslims.
- To explain what the roles of prophets teach Muslims.
- To explore specifically the examples of Adam, Ibrahim, Isma'il, Musa, Dawud, Isa and Muhammad.

Risalah in Islam

Risalah literally means 'message' in **Arabic**. Muslims believe that it is the communication channel between Allah and humanity. They believe that Allah gave messages to Nubuwwah, prophets, or messengers, and thereby revealed himself and his word. This is called **revelation**. The messages that Allah sent to the prophets are recorded in the Islamic holy books and the religion is based on these messages.

Muslim tradition states that there have been 124,000 prophets in total. The Qur'an names 25 prophets, many of whom also appear in the holy books of Judaism and Christianity.

Muslims recognise that the prophets were chosen by Allah to reveal his truth and therefore should be shown respect. They do not, however, worship the prophets because they believe that Allah is the one true god and only he is worthy of worship. Whenever Muslims mention any of the prophets, they say 'peace be upon him' as a sign of respect. Muslims believe that Allah sent his messages to the prophets via Malaikah, the angels. While some prophets simply give messages, other prophets called **rasuls** were given holy books, or scripture, where their messages were written down. Belief in prophethood is therefore closely linked to the Six Beliefs of Islam as prophethood is often understood to be the source of how these beliefs were given to humanity.

Some of the prophets are listed below. Some are important in other religions, for example, Ibrahim and Isa are significant to the Jewish and Christian religions.

Qur'anic name	Biblical name
Adam	Adam
Nuh	Noah
Ibrahim	Abraham
Isma'il	Ishmael
Ishaq	Isaac
Yusuf	Joseph
Musa	Moses
Dawud	David
Sulayman	Solomon
Yunus	Jonah
Yahya	John
Isa	Jesus

What do the roles of prophets teach Muslims?

Muslims believe that all the prophets brought the same message: that Allah called people to worship him as the one true god. However, many messengers were needed as the message was distorted or ignored. Muslims accept that prophets are the link between Allah and humanity, and this is how Allah revealed what he is like and how he wants people to live.

Muslims believe that the role of the prophets teaches them that:

- Allah loves them and wants to communicate with them through people and holy books
- Allah wants to share his message about how he wants them to live
- humanity is important to Allah and he is omnipresent, watching over them.

Sources of authority

Say: "We believe in Allah, and the revelation given to us, and to Abraham, Ismail, Isaac, Jacob, and the Tribes, and that given to Moses and Jesus, and that given to (all) prophets from their Lord: we make no difference between one and another of them: and we bow to Allah (in Islam)." (Surah 2:136)

Adam

Muslims believe that Adam was the first Muslim as well as the first prophet. Allah created Adam as the first human and gave him the role of **khalifah**, meaning looking after the world. This is a key idea within the Qur'an and Muslims claim this responsibility is a duty that they should perform within the world, caring for what Allah has created and provided. Muslims believe that they can learn about their role on Earth from the example of Adam.

Ibrahim

Islam is an Abrahamic religion. This means it has a lot in common with Christianity and Judaism, as they both recognise the prophet known as Abraham. In Islam he is known as Ibrahim, and he is seen by Muslims as the father of the Arab people, as well as the Jewish people through his two sons – Isaac and Isma'il. The story of Ibrahim having his faith tested by God by being asked to sacrifice his son teaches Muslims to be prepared to submit to Allah, just as Ibrahim was willing to do. Muslims believe that Ibrahim brought a scripture to humanity (the Scrolls of Abraham), although these are now believed to be lost.

Isma'il

Isma'il is one of Ibrahim's two sons. He is regarded as a prophet and an ancestor of Muhammad. Muslims believe that Isma'il was associated with Makkah and the construction of the **Ka'bah**, the sacred shrine in Makkah, which all Muslims face when they pray.

Musa

Musa is seen by Muslims as a prophet who taught and practised the religion of his ancestors, thereby confirming the scriptures and prophets who came before him. The Qur'an states that Musa was sent by Allah to give guidance to the pharaoh of Egypt and the Israelites. Israel holds religious significance for Muslims as a number of key prophets prior to Muhammad were associated with the land.

Dawud

Dawud is recognised by Muslims as a prophet, leader and law-giver of Allah. He is known in Islam for defeating Goliath when he was a soldier. Goliath was a fighter who challenged any soldier in single combat. Dawud, a youth from Bethlehem, was initially mocked for standing to fight Goliath until, using his slingshot, he killed Goliath before he could even raise his sword. The Psalms of Dawud are referred to in the Qur'an as having been revealed to him by Allah, and are recognised as one of the holy books of Islam. Dawud is recognised as a prophet who brought the message from Allah to humanity before to Muhammad.

Isa

Isa is mentioned in 15 chapters of the Qur'an, showing his importance as a prophet. In Christianity he is called Jesus. Muslims recognise his miraculous virgin birth to Mary, but do not accept that he died on the cross or was resurrected, as Christians do. Muslims refer to Isa as the 'son of Mary' rather than the 'son of God', as they view him as a human being only. They believe that there is only one god in Allah, and so Isa cannot be divine. Muslims understand the stories of Isa from the Gospels, which are part of the Christian holy book, the Bible. Not all Muslims accept the stories as true; many think they have been corrupted throughout time, and that Allah's original message has been altered.

Muhammad, the last prophet

Muhammad is seen as the final prophet and is often considered the founder of Islam. He is referred to as

Figure 1.4 The cave on Mount Hira where Muhammad is believed to have received his revelations

18

the 'Seal of the Prophets' as he is accepted as the final messenger and his message from Allah is contained in the Qur'an. Muslims accept that this is the complete message to humanity, and the central beliefs of Islam are based on it. The message was revealed to Muhammad by the **Archangel Jibril** in a cave on **Mount Hira**, over a period of 23 years. He remembered the message and later recited it to his people. It was compiled in the Qur'an after Muhammad's death, but it has remained unchanged since that time. The Arabic word Qur'an literally means 'recitation' and Muslims believe it is important to keep the Qur'an in its original language of Arabic so as not to lose any of its meaning. This is why Muslims learn the Qur'an in Arabic. Muslims believe that the first religious leaders were direct descendants of Muhammad.

Can you remember?

- What are the Six Beliefs of Islam for Sunni Muslims and how is Risalah one of these key beliefs?
- Why are these beliefs are so important to Sunni Muslims?
- How do Muslims express their beliefs about Risalah in their daily lives?

Exam-style questions

Explain two reasons why prophets are important in Islam.
(4 marks)

Exam tip

This question requires you to give two different reasons. Make sure you explain them both fully, using examples if possible to show your understanding of why they are important.

Activities ?

1. Make a list of the characteristics a good teacher should have. Why do you think these are needed? Do you think the prophets would have had these characteristics? Why or why not?
2. In groups, imagine that you have been asked to host a 'Question Time' interview with a selection of the prophets. Plan the questions you would ask them and say how you think they might respond. Once you have planned it, role play your interview.
3. Write an answer to the question, 'Why does the fact there are so many prophets show that Allah cares for humanity?'

Summary

- Risalah, the belief in the communication of messages from Allah through the prophets, is very important to Muslims.
- Nubuwwah, or prophets, are the messengers of Allah and the connection between Allah and humanity.
- Some prophets have simply brought messages, while others have been trusted to bring sources of authority in the form of holy books.
- Muslims recognise many prophets who are also seen in the other Abrahamic religions, such as Judaism and Christianity.

Checkpoint

Strengthen

S1 Where do Muslims get their information about the prophets from?

S2 Name four prophets who are important to Islam and explain why they are important.

S3 Why is Muhammad so important to the religion of Islam?

Challenge

C1 Why do you think revelation is so important to Muslims?

C2 What can we learn today from the examples of the prophets?

C3 Why do you think some people living in the time of the prophets did not accept the messages they were giving?

1.5 Muslim holy books (kutub)

Learning objectives

- To understand the nature and history of holy books in Islam.
- To explore the significance of holy books in Islam.
- To identify the importance and purpose of Muslim holy books today.

Kutub is taken to mean 'revealed books' as they are revealed to humanity from Allah.

The Qur'an

The main holy book for Muslims is the Qur'an. Muslims believe that it was revealed to the Prophet Muhammad over 23 years through the Angel Jibril and that the words came directly from Allah. Unusual as this may have seemed to non-believers, Surah 53:4–18 assures that these are not the words of a liar or an insane person, but the true message of Allah revealed to Muhammad. Muslims believe that Muhammad recited the words told to him by the Angel Jibril his followers and that it was written down on scraps of writing material or committed to memory. They were collected into a book immediately after Muhammad's death, under the direction of Abu Bakr, who succeeded Muhammad. Uthman, Muhammad's third successor, then standardised copies and all copies since then have been identical.

The Qur'an is written in Arabic and Muslims believe it is important to read, understand and learn it in its original language, so that its meaning can be understood fully and does not get changed through translation.

Figure 1.5 The Qu'ran – the holy book of Islam

The Qur'an is divided into **surahs**, or chapters, and each of these is made up of **ayats**, or verses. It is organised according to length, with the longest chapter at the start and shortest at the end. Many Muslims learn the Qur'an by heart and as a mark of respect they are then called **hafiz** if male and **hafizah** if female. This is done as a reminder that this is the format in which the Qur'an was revealed to Muhammad. It is considered a challenge to be able to recite the Qur'an so great respect is given to those who can achieve this.

How do Muslims show respect to the Qur'an?

Muslims believe the Qur'an came directly from Allah and that therefore it deserves respect. They show this by:

- not allowing it to touch the ground – it will be placed on a **kursi**, a Qur'an stand usually made out of wood, when it is read
- washing before they read it to ensure they are clean
- not handling the Qur'an unless absolutely necessary
- not speaking, eating or drinking when reading the words of Allah
- covering it to protect it when it is not used
- placing it at the highest point in the room to signify that it is above all other possessions.

Other holy books

The Qur'an mentions four other holy books: the Tawrat, Zabur, Injil and Sahifah of Ibrahim. All the holy books are 'kutub', which is taken to mean 'revealed books' as they are revealed to humanity from Allah. Muslims believe the four other holy books originally contained the same message as the Qur'an. However, they believe their meaning has been gradually changed or corrupted over time, suggesting they became a mixture of Allah's words alongside those added by humans. Muslims therefore only accept the Qur'an as the true word of Allah and the most important of his revelations.

The **Tawrat** – the Torah *Surah 5:43–48*	According to the Qur'an, the Tawrat, the Jewish holy book, was revealed to Moses. They accept this is the longest-used scripture. While Jews still use it today, Muslims believe it has become corrupted over the years and is no longer reliable, but recognition of it teaches Muslims that Allah had previous messengers to Muhammad.
Zabur – Psalms of Dawud (David) *Surah 4: 163–171*	The Qur'an mentions the Zabur as being the scripture revealed to King David. The current Psalms are still recognised by many Muslim scholars but some believe they were not divinely revealed.
Injil – the Gospel of Isa (Jesus) *Surah 53:36*	The Qur'an recognises the Injil as the book revealed to Isa. Muslims believe its meaning has been altered over time and therefore Allah's words have been changed. It teaches Muslims about the revelations that they believed were revealed by Allah to Isa.
Sahifah of Ibrahim – Scrolls of Abraham *Surah 6:74–83*	Many Muslims believe these were an early scripture revealed to Ibrahim and used by his sons Isma'il and Isaac. They are considered today by Islam to be lost rather than corrupted. They teach Muslims what Allah revealed to Prophet Ibrahim.

Why are holy books important in Islam today?

- All Muslims believe Allah is behind the messages they contain and therefore they are a form of revelation about Allah, showing Muslims what Allah is like.
- Muslims believe that holy books contain truths from Allah and therefore should not be questioned nor altered – Muslims believe they should submit to Allah, and this includes his words in holy books.
- The books, especially the Qur'an, which is considered to be Allah's final revelation, guide Muslims in how Allah wants them to live.
- The books show that Allah wants to interact with his creation, specifically humans.
- Muslims believe they can get closer to Allah and understand him better by reading his words.
- Although some Muslims may place more emphasis on holy books than others, they all believe that they are important as a source of authority and wisdom.
- Some Muslims may prefer simply to recognise the Qur'an, as this is understood to be the final and complete message from Allah, which has been unaltered.
- Other Muslims may wish to read and understand the holy books mentioned in this section, as well as the Qur'an, as it will help them to gain a better understanding of Allah and his purpose for them in the world.

Sources of authority

Nay, is he not acquainted with what is in the books of Moses(?)
(Surah 53:36)

We have sent you inspiration, as We sent it to Noah and the Messengers after him: We sent inspiration to Abraham, Ismā'īl, Isaac, Jacob and the Tribes, to Jesus, Job, Jonah, Aaron, and Solomon, and to David We gave the Psalms.
(Surah 4:163)

And in their footsteps We sent Jesus the son of Mary, confirming the Law that had come before him: We sent him the Gospel: therein was guidance and light, and confirmation of the Law that had come before him: a guidance and an admonition to those who fear Allah.
(Surah 5:46)

Activities ?

1 What is your favourite book? Share it with a partner, giving a brief synopsis of the story. Explain three reasons why you like this book and why it is important to you.

2 Explain why Muslims feel it is so important to show respect to the Qur'an. Think of an example of how you show respect to something in your life. Make a list of ways in which you do this.

3 Imagine you have been asked to talk to a group of non-Muslims about the Qur'an, explaining what it is and why it is important. Plan what you would say and write a speech.

Activities ?

4 In a group, discuss the advantages and disadvantages of using the Qur'an today as a source of authority. Think about reasons why some people may suggest it is too old or out of date, while others may argue that the teachings it contains are timeless and still relevant. Make sure you use examples in your arguments.

Exam-style questions

Explain two reasons why holy books are important in Islam today. In your answer you must refer to a source of wisdom and authority. **(5 marks)**

Exam tip

You will be awarded one mark for each reason that you offer (two are required) and a second mark if you can develop each reason fully. This style of question also requires you to make reference to a source of wisdom or authority in order to achieve the final mark.

Extend your knowledge

There are 114 surahs, or chapters, in the Qur'an. Each surah has a name that is taken from the beginning of the chapter or a significant word within the chapter. All surahs except Surah 9 begin with the words 'Bismillah-ir Rahman-ir-Rahim', which means 'In the Name of Allah, the Merciful Benefactor, The Merciful Redeemer.'

Sources of authority

That this is indeed a Qur'an Most honourable, In Book well-guarded, Which none shall touch but those who are clean: A Revelation from the Lord of the Worlds. (Surah 56:77–80)

I leave behind me two things, the Qur'an and my example the Sunnah and if you follow these you will never go astray. (Prophet Muhammad's last sermon)

Summary

- Holy books, or kutub, are important to Muslims.
- Muslims recognise the Tawrah, Zabur, Injil, Sahifah and the Qur'an as holy books.
- The Qur'an is considered to be the most important as it is the final, complete revelation from Allah.
- Holy books are a way Allah communicates with humanity and they are sources of authority and guidance for Muslims.
- Muslims believe their holy books are as important today as when they were first revealed.

Checkpoint

Strengthen

S1 Can you name the holy books identified and accepted by Muslims?

S2 Why is the Qur'an considered to be the most important holy book for Muslims?

S3 Why are holy books important for Muslims today?

Challenge

C1 Why do you think Muslims feel it is important to learn the Qur'an by heart?

C2 Why do you think Muslims feel it is important to show respect to the Qur'an at all times?

C3 When do you think Muslims might use the Qur'an?

1.6 Malaikah: angels

Learning objectives

- To understand the nature and importance of angels for Muslims.
- To be able to explain how the angels Jibril, Izra'il and Mika'il are shown in the Qur'an.
- To explore the significance of angels for Muslims today.

Islam and angels

Islam believes strongly in the existence of angels; indeed, they are recognised as one of the Six Beliefs for Sunni Muslims. They believe that although Allah is the only spiritual being that should be worshipped, other **supernatural** beings which are beyond the physical world, Malaikah or angels, are the servants of Allah. They believe that angels were created from light and have no physical body of their own, but they can appear in human form. Muslims also accept that angels have no free will, so they can only do what Allah orders them to do.

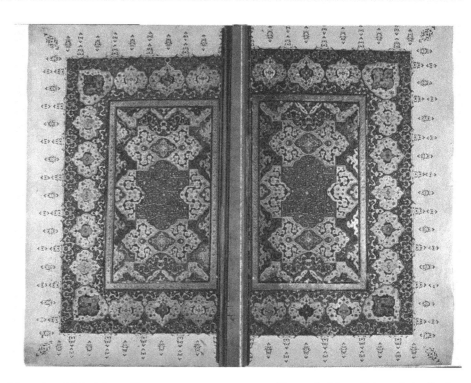

Figure 1.6 An edition of the Qur'an

Angels are also seen to have a guardianship role within Islam. They are believed to have accompanied Muhammad up to al-Jannah where he received commands from Allah. Angels are also seen to be used by Allah in other ways, such as overseeing al-Jannah. It is also believed that there are angels who oversee the clouds and give life to unborn children in their mother's womb. The angels perform all of these tasks at Allah's command.

Muslims recognise that there will be a Day of Judgement after death. It is taught in Islam that at this time the end of the world will come and humans will be judged on their actions and deeds on Earth. In order that this can be done, Muslims are taught that throughout their lives, there are two angels present. One writes down their good deeds while the other writes down their bad deeds. This information is then used to make the decision on whether each person deserves to go to al-Jannah or to be punished in Jahannam, or Hell. In this way, angels hold very important roles for Allah.

Muhammad is believed to have told followers that angels surround humans at all times and present a full report on each and every human after death to Allah. Some angels are given special importance by Allah and hold roles of significance in the world. They are mentioned in the Qur'an and therefore given recognition and importance by Muslims today.

Sources of authority

The Messenger believes in what has been revealed to him from his Lord, as do the men of faith. Each one (of them) believes in Allah, His angels, His books, and His Messengers. "We make no distinction (they say) between one and another of His Messengers." And they say: "We hear, and we obey: (we seek) Your forgiveness, our Lord, and to You is the end of all journeys."
(Surah 2:285)

Angels in the Qur'an and their importance

Some angels are given higher ranks than other angels and are known as **archangels**. Three archangels identified on numerous occasions in the Qur'an and accepted as important to all Muslims are:

- Jibril, or Gabriel as he is known in Judaism and Christianity, is given the role in Islam of revealing messages from Allah to the prophets, most notably revealing the Qur'an to Muhammad

- Izra'il, who is given the important role of blowing the trumpet twice to signal the start of the Day of Judgement according to the Qur'an – the first blow will bring all humankind to attention and end all life, while the second will return all humans back to life to face Allah and be judged

- Mika'il, recognised in Christianity and Judaism as Michael, is often shown as the archangel of mercy – he is believed to bring rain and thunder to Earth and is seen to be the one who is responsible for giving out rewards to people who are good.

These angels are seen by Muslims to have been given roles of importance by Allah and should therefore be respected and remembered. Muslims believe that Allah chooses to communicate with them, as depicted for example in Surah 19, and the angels are considered important because of this.

What is the significance of angels for Muslims today?

Belief in Malaikah is a compulsory act, a requirement of being a Muslim, as it forms part of the Six Beliefs of Islam for Sunni Muslims. It is important for Muslims today for several reasons.

- This belief helps Muslims to understand Allah better – the angels are the creations of Allah and therefore reveal truths to Muslims, such as Allah wanting to communicate with humanity and using the angels to pass messages to the prophets.

- Muslims feel a sense of awe and amazement towards Allah as they believe he is transcendent but has been able to communicate with humanity using the angels.

- Jibril is the angel who was used to reveal the Qur'an to Muhammad. As Muhammad is accepted to have

brought the final, perfect message from Allah, he is of particular importance.

- Izra'il and Mika'il are associated with what happens after death for Muslims – something that will also affect how they live. The roles of these angels remind Muslims of the importance of living as Allah wants them to, in order to be rewarded after death.

Activities ?

1. Imagine you have been given the privilege of meeting any of the three angels mentioned on these pages. Explain who you would want to meet and why, including explanation of what you would ask them and why.

2. Discuss with a partner whether angels watching what humans do and reporting on it is a good or bad thing.

3. How and why do you think a belief in angels will affect the life of a Muslim? Write an explanation your thoughts, making sure you give examples where appropriate.

Sources of authority

Say: Whoever is an enemy to Gabriel – for he brings down the (revelation) to your heart by Allah's will, a confirmation of what went before, and guidance and glad tidings for those who believe, –

Whoever is an enemy to Allah and His angels and messengers, to Gabriel and Michael, – Lo! Allah is an enemy to those who reject Faith.
(Surah 2:97–98)

… then We sent to her Our angel, and he appeared before her as a man in all respects.
(Surah, 19:17)

Say: "The Angel of Death, put in charge of you, will (duly) take your souls: then shall you be brought back to your Lord." (Surah 32:11)

Can you remember?

- What are the Six Beliefs of Islam?
- Why are the Six Beliefs of Islam important?
- How do the Six Beliefs of Islam affect the life of a Muslim today?

Exam-style questions

Explain two reasons why angels are important in Islam. In your answer, you must refer to a source of wisdom and authority. **(5 marks)**

Exam tip

You need to demonstrate your knowledge accurately, making sure you explain each reason you give before moving onto the next one. The question also requires you to refer to a source of wisdom or authority within your answer to achieve the fifth mark available.

Summary

- Malaikah is an important belief in Islam – it is one of the Six Beliefs.
- Muslims believe angels were created by Allah and are used as his servants.
- Three angels, Jibril, Izra'il and Mika'il, are given special importance in Islam.
- Muslims believe that angels are important today and will have an impact on how they live.

Checkpoint

Strengthen

S1 What is Malaikah?

S2 Who are the three main angels in Islam and what roles are they given?

S3 Where do Muslims get their knowledge about angels from and why is this important?

Challenge

C1 Give three examples of how a Muslim's life might be affected by the knowledge of the existence of angels.

C2 What do you think we can learn about Allah from each of the archangels – Jibril, Izra'il and Mika'il?

C3 Why might some people say there is no evidence to suggest that angels exist?

1.7 Al-Qadr: predestination

Learning objectives

- To understand the nature and importance of predestination for Muslims.
- To identify how al-Qadr and human freedom relates to the Day of Judgement.
- To consider the implications of belief in al-Qadr for Muslims today.

What is al-Qadr and why is it important?

Al-Qadr is the Islamic idea of predestination, the idea that Allah has control over everything and knows everything that will come to pass before it happens. This is a belief accepted by Sunni Muslims but not by Shi'a Muslims. Some Muslims believe that Allah has written down everything that has happened and that will happen. They do not believe that a person's actions will occur because Allah has decided it, but that he already knows and has recorded what choices they will make with their free will. It is one of the Six Beliefs for Sunni Muslims. They believe that although Allah gave humans free will, he is omnipotent, all-powerful, and **omniscient**, all-knowing, and controls the destiny of every person. Muslims accept that nothing happens unless it is the will of Allah and they often use the words 'Insha allah', meaning 'If Allah is willing', to show that they submit to this.

Belief in predestination is based on four things: Allah's knowledge of everything that has been and will be, the idea that Allah has recorded these, that everything that does happen is willed by Allah, and finally that Allah is the creator of everything. Some people may raise questions about the apparent conflict between some of these ideas. Muslims believe that although Allah is aware of what is going to happen, he does not

Figure 1.7 Muslims believe that they must submit to the will of Allah. During prayer, they prostrate themselves to the floor to show this

interfere. This is because Muslims also accept that Allah gave humans free will and to be involved in the world would mean Allah was violating this idea. Although Allah does not want people to make the wrong decisions, he accepts that sometimes this is what needs to happen in order for humans to have free will – without free will they cannot completely and willingly submit to Allah. The belief in al-Qadr comes from the Qur'an. For instance, passages such as Surah 11:110 suggest that believers should wait patiently for the consequences of people misbehaving towards Allah as He has already ordained what will happen to them.

Al-Qadr and human freedom

Muslims accept the teaching of al-Qadr, but it may be more difficult for others to understand why, if Allah is controlling everything that happens and knows what will happen, he doesn't prevent bad things from taking place. Islam holds that Allah gave humans free will when he created them. This means that humans have choices and can decide what to do in any given situation. Therefore humans are responsible for their own sins, as they have decided what action to take.

Muslims believe that Allah knows every human so well that he knows what they will choose before they make the decision for themselves. They accept that every human has a purpose given to them by Allah and they can choose to go along with this divine purpose or reject it and turn away from Allah. Muslims believe that on the Day of Judgement, all mankind will be destroyed and then brought back to life to be judged by Allah. They are accountable for their own actions and Allah judges whether they should be punished or rewarded. Although Allah knows the choices they made, the human beings were still free to choose otherwise. In this way, there is no contradiction between the ideas of al-Qadr and human freedom.

Differences between Sunni and Shi'a beliefs about predestination

Sunni and Shi'a Muslims hold slightly different beliefs about predestination. Some Shi'a Muslims, such as the Twelvers, reject the idea of predestination. Instead they accept that Allah is in control, but he may decide to change what happens. However, most Shi'a Muslims emphasise human free will, understanding predestination simply as Allah having the foreknowledge of how a person will act. In contrast, Sunni Muslims tend to emphasise the idea of Divine

Sovereignty, believing that, although humans have the choice to decide what they do, Allah already knows the decision they will make. This can be associated with the phrase "If Allah wills…" which Sunni Muslims understand very literally as if Allah wants something, that is what happens.

What are the implications for belief in al-Qadr for Muslims today?

Muslims live in the knowledge of al-Qadr. It helps them make sense of the world around them – if Allah knows everything and has control of all things that happen it must mean that events happen for a reason. Belief in al-Qadr affects their lives because:

- they want to be rewarded rather than punished after death, so they try to live in the way Allah wants
- they try to follow the duties given to them by Allah
- they try to help others, as this is what the Qur'an and Muhammad's example teach them to do
- they try to constantly be aware of their thoughts, actions and deeds to ensure they are living by the rules of Allah.

Sources of authority

Nor can a soul die except by Allah's leave…
(Surah 3:145)

The Prophet said, "Allah says, 'The vow, does not bring about for the son of Adam anything I have not decreed for him, but his vow may coincide with what has been decided for him, and by this way I cause a miser to spend of his wealth. So he gives Me (spends in charity) for the fulfillment of what has been decreed for him what he would not give Me before but for his vow."
(Hadith (Sahih Al-Bukhari) 78:685)

Activities

1 Explain five ways in which you show submission towards your friends and family. Share your ideas with a partner. If you were to accept ideas about al-Qadr or predestination, would you live your life any differently? Explain reasons for your answer.

2 Explain what evidence there is that humans have free will in their lives. As an extension, explain Muslim views about this.

Exam-style questions

'It is not possible to accept the ideas of al-Qadr and human free will.' Evaluate this statement, considering arguments for and against. In your response you should:

- refer to Muslim teachings
- reach a justified conclusion.

(15 marks)

Activities

3 'We should make the most of life now and not worry about the future.' Create a table of arguments agreeing and disagreeing with this statement. Discuss them with a partner and debate which side of the argument you think is strongest and why.

Exam tip

This question asks you to consider a range of viewpoints about the given statement. Before you start writing your answer, think about what different people might say – would they agree or disagree? What reason might they give? Make sure you include Muslim views in your answer, and that you show awareness of any diversity that exists between different Muslim groups.

Extend your knowledge

There are differences between Sunni and Shi'a acceptance of the idea of al-Qadr. Sunni Muslims hold it to be true – this can be seen by the fact they show its importance by having it as one of the Six Beliefs in Sunni Islam. In contrast, Shi'a Muslims reject the idea of predestination. This is further reinforced by acceptance of the Shi'a concept of Bada', which states that God has not set a definite course for humans.

Summary

- Al-Qadr is the Islamic belief in predestination – that Allah controls everything.
- Every aspect of being a Muslim follows the idea of submission to Allah.
- Muslims believe that al-Qadr and human free will do not contradict each other but work together.
- Belief in al-Qadr will affect the daily life of a Muslim in how they act and behave.

Checkpoint

Strengthen

S1 Why do Muslims feel that a belief in al-Qadr is important?

S2 How do you think the quotes in the Sources of authority box reflect the idea of al-Qadr?

S3 Why do Muslims believe that al-Qadr and human free will can work together?

Challenge

C1 In your own words, explain what you think a Muslim can learn from a belief in al-Qadr.

C2 How might a belief in al-Qadr impact on humans living in the modern world?

C3 Why might many people not accept the belief of predestination?

1.8 Akhirah: life after death

Learning objectives

- To explore Muslim teachings about life after death.
- To understand the nature of judgement, paradise and hell, and how they are seen in the Qur'an.
- To consider how Muslim teachings about life after death affect the life of a Muslim.

Islam and Akhirah

Belief in life after death is fundamental to Islam. It features in both the Sunni Six Beliefs and Shi'a Five Roots of 'Usul ad-Din. Muslims believe life on Earth is only part of human existence, as it continues after death. Life on Earth is our chance to live good lives as Allah intended or to choose to turn our back on Allah and his laws. Muslims believe that after death every human will be called to answer for the way they have lived their life and that this will affect their afterlife, determining whether they will be rewarded or punished. Muslims accept belief in Akhirah because it was promised by Allah, and they believe he never breaks his promises.

Muslims believe that at each person's death, two angels will visit them and record their good and bad deeds to decide whether they are fit to enter paradise. The angels are believed to ask questions such as, 'Who is your god?', 'What is your religion?' and 'Who is your prophet?' How a person answers these questions will determine their future life in the afterlife, alongside how they acted in their life on Earth. They believe that there will be a Day of Judgement, when there will be a complete resurrection of the body and all deeds will be judged by Allah. Prior to this day, they believe that the souls of the dead will go to **Barzakh**, which is understood as a barrier between the physical and spiritual worlds, where they will wait until the Day of Judgement.

Muslims believe that those who succeed in the test on the Day of Judgement will be rewarded with paradise, al-Jannah, while those who fail will suffer in hell, or Jahannam.

What does the Qur'an say?

The Qur'an offers vivid images of life after death. It talks of the end of the world being where stars will scatter, mountains tumble, oceans boil over and the dead will be raised from their tombs. Good and bad deeds will be weighed and each person will have to face Allah. Paradise and hell are described in the Qur'an as physical states, although many Muslims believe that this is symbolic, because eternal life is beyond human understanding.

Al-Jannah

Al-Jannah, or paradise, is described in the Qur'an as a wonderful garden. People are thought to return to their young states and be able to enjoy all the pleasures the garden offers. The Qur'an includes reference to flowers, birds and fruit served by youths and maidens. Reference is made to couches or thrones with soft cushions, and goblets and dishes made from gold. Paradise is seen as a reward and a place of beauty.

Sources of authority

"Did you then think that We had created you in jest and that you would not be brought back to Us (for account)?"
(Surah 23:115)

Fruits (Delights)… In Gardens of Felicity… Thrones… a clear-flowing fountain, Crystal-white, of a taste delicious to those who drink (thereof).
(Surah 37:42–46)

Figure 1.8 Al-Jannah is a beautiful garden that awaits Muslims that pass the test on the Day of Judgement, according to the Qur'an

Sources of authority

Therefore do I warn you of a Fire blazing fiercely; none shall reach it but those most unfortunate ones Who gave the lie to truth and turn their backs. But those most devoted to Allah shall be removed far from it. (Surah 92:14–17)

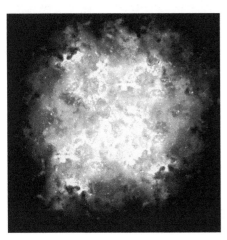

Figure 1.9 Muslims believe that those who don't go to paradise will end up in Jahannam

Can you remember?

- What is the role of Akhirah in the Six Beliefs of Islam and Five Roots of 'Usul ad-Din?
- What are the characteristics of Allah and how are they shown in ideas of Akhirah?
- What is the link between Akhirah, al-Qadr and judgement?

Jahannam

In contrast, Jahannam is a place of hell; of fire, black smoke and boiling water. It is seen as a place of punishment where those who deserve it face endless pain and torture – a fitting punishment for those who chose to turn away from Allah.

Allah and judgement

Muslims believe that Allah is not evil and that punishment through Jahannam is not because he is a cruel tyrant. They accept that because Allah gave humans free will, some will choose to turn away from him. The fate of these people is inevitable, as they have used their free will to turn away from Allah and must face the consequences, as depicted in Surah 17:49–72.

How will beliefs about Akhirah affect the life of a Muslim?

Akhirah is such an important belief to Muslims that it is bound to affect their lives in some way. They see their life on Earth as a test from Allah, and obviously want to be rewarded in the afterlife, so this may make them think about their beliefs, actions and behaviour.

Muslims will try to live their lives as Allah wants them to. This might take different forms, but most Muslims will try to:

- be more aware of their lives – their thoughts, actions and deeds are being watched by Allah and recorded by the angels, so it may make them think more carefully about these
- realise the importance of asking for forgiveness when they do something wrong, as they know Allah will also see and hear this
- be more aware that every action they perform is an act of worship to Allah
- try to please Allah by performing sacred duties, reading the Qur'an, following **Shari'ah law**, caring for those around them, being honest and faithful and working hard.

Similarities and differences between Islam and Christianity

Beliefs about the afterlife are important to both Muslims and Christians. They both:

- view life as a test in terms of determining their afterlife
- hold beliefs in a place of eternal reward and a place of eternal punishment, alongside the idea of a Day of Judgement
- share ideas in regards to resurrection.

Differences include how:

- Christians accept the sacrifice of Jesus to atone for the sins of the world but Muslims believe only the sinner themselves can ask for forgiveness
- some Christians, such as Catholics, accept the idea of purgatory, alongside heaven and hell, which is not seen in Islam
- Muslims accept ideas of angels who record the deeds of a person whereas Christians do not.

Sources of authority

Does man think that We cannot assemble his bones? Nay, We are able to put together in perfect order the very tips of his fingers. (Surah 75:3–4)

Then when the Trumpet is blown, there will be no more relationships between them that Day, nor will one ask after another! (Surah 23: 101)

Activities ?

1 Explain that what you believe about death and why. Share your thoughts with a partner to see whether you agree or disagree. Does it matter if you don't agree?

2 Read the descriptions in the Sources of authority box of al-Jannah and Jahannam. Why do you think Muslims offer such physical descriptions of these places? Do you think it is the right thing to do to offer physical descriptions? Why or why not?

3 Imagine you are having an email conversation with a friend who is a Muslim. Write both sides of the conversation to show you understand the Muslim view and an alternative view of what happens after death. Make sure you explain ideas fully and develop the points you make by including examples.

Exam-style questions

In this question, 3 of the marks awarded will be for your spelling, punctuation and grammar and your use of specialist terminology.

'Death is just the end and that is that – there is no evidence of Paradise and Hell.' Evaluate this statement considering arguments for and against. In your response you should

• refer to Muslim teachings
• reach a justified conclusion.
   (15 marks)

Exam tip

Death and the afterlife are complex topics and you need to demonstrate that you understand this in your answer. Make sure you think of a number of arguments agreeing and disagreeing with the statement, explaining each fully. Examiners require you to demonstrate thorough knowledge and understanding of this topic to access the highest possible marks, as well as show awareness of diversity of views.

Summary

• Akhirah is the Islamic word for life after death.
• Muslims believe this life is a test for the afterlife.
• The Qur'an is where Muslims get their information about the afterlife.
• If they have lived their life as Allah wants, they will go to al-Jannah, paradise.
• If they have not lived their life as Allah has required, they will go to Jahannam, hell.
• Muslim beliefs about the afterlife will impact on the way a Muslim lives their life.

Checkpoint

Strengthen

S1 What is Akhirah and where do Muslims gain their knowledge about it from?

S2 Can you explain what Muslims believe about al-Jannah and Jahannam?

S3 Why is Allah not seen as evil for allowing some people to be punished?

Challenge

C1 In your own words, can you explain why Akhirah is important to Muslims?

C2 Why do you think Muslims are so aware of Akhirah and judgement?

C3 Can you explain why some people may not accept that there is an afterlife?

Recap: Muslim beliefs

The activities on the next two pages will help you to remember the things you have learned before you move on to the next chapter. It is important that you consolidate your knowledge about Muslim teachings and beliefs as this will assist your understanding of the other topics in this book – Living the Muslim life, Crime and punishment, and Peace and conflict.

Recap quiz

The Six Beliefs of Islam

1   Name each of the Six Beliefs of Islam for Sunni Muslims.
2   How are the Six Beliefs of Islam for Sunni Muslims put into practice in everyday life?

The Five Roots of 'Usul ad-Din in Shi'a Islam

3   Name each of the Five Roots of 'Usul ad-Din for Shi'a Muslims.
4   How are the Five Roots of 'Usul ad-Din for Shi'a Muslims put into practice in everyday life?
5   What are the key differences between Sunni and Shi'a Muslims?

The nature of Allah

6   State five characteristics of Allah.
7   Name five of the 99 names of Allah.
8   How are beliefs about Allah seen to be central to the religion of Islam?

Risalah: prophethood

9   What is Risalah?
10 Name four prophets accepted by Muslims.
11 Who is Muhammad?
12 Why is Muhammad so important to Muslims?
13 What can Muslims today learn from the prophets?

Muslim holy books

14 Name the holy books recognised by Muslims.
15 What is the most important holy book for Muslims called?
16 Why do Muslims accept a number of holy books?
17 Why is the Qur'an considered to be so important to Muslims?

Malaikah: angels

18 What are Malaikah?
19 Name three angels recognised by Muslims.
20 Why would Islam not exist without the angels?

Al-Qadr: predestination

21 What is al-Qadr and how is it differently interpreted by Sunnis and Shi'as?
22 Why is a belief in predestination so important to Sunni Muslims and how does it relate to ideas of Tawhid?

Akhirah: life after death

23 What is Akhirah?
24 How do beliefs about Akhirah affect the daily life of Muslims?
25 Give five examples of how a Muslim might live according to all their beliefs.

Exam-style questions

- Outline three Muslim beliefs about judgement. **(3 marks**)

- Explain two reasons why Risalah is important to Muslims. **(4 marks)**

- Explain two reasons why belief in Tawhid is essential for Muslims. In your answer you must refer to a source of wisdom and authority. **(5 marks)**

- In this question, 3 of the marks awarded will be for your spelling, punctuation and grammar and your use of specialist terminology. 'The Qur'an is the most important source of authority for Muslims.' Evaluate this statement, considering arguments for and against. In your response you should
  - ° refer to Muslim teachings
  - ° reach a justified conclusion. **(15 marks)**

Activities

1. Create a spider diagram showing what beliefs are essential to being a Muslim and following the Islamic faith.

2. Create a set of flashcards – one for each of the key terms studied in this chapter. Write the key term on one side and its meaning and examples on the other.

3. 'It is easy to live as a Muslim today.' Consider this statement and create a table of arguments for and against. Share your arguments with a partner to develop them. Have a class debate about this statement.

4. Imagine you are on the radio and are interviewing a group of Muslims about their faith. Use all the knowledge you have gained in this chapter to write a series of questions that you can give to a partner. Get them to answer your questions. Record your interview to use in your revision.

5. In groups, think about what it means to be a Muslim. Consider things in their lives they may find easy and things they may find difficult. Write a speech explaining how you think they might feel about their religion.

Exam tips

- Each question has a 'command' word that instructs you in what you are required to do. Make sure you look at this carefully to ensure you understand what the question is asking.

- Read each question carefully before starting to answer it. If appropriate, plan your answer carefully to decide what knowledge is important to include.

- Make sure you practise each style of question carefully to familiarise yourself with how you should answer it.

- When giving different views, make sure you support each one with at least two different reasons.

- Remember that you have to demonstrate your knowledge and show you understand how ideas are related to each other in your work. Remember to return to your prior knowledge and topics you have covered in other chapters to do this.

- Make sure that when you are trying to persuade people of your view that it is important to use persuasive language. You need to always check that what you have written suits the purpose it is intended for.

Extend: Muslim beliefs

Source

Hello, my name is Rayan. I am a Muslim and this means I follow the religion of Islam. I will tell you a little bit about my faith. I believe in one God and call him Allah. I pray to him five times every day – sometimes with my family and sometimes alone. I also try to attend the Mosque on a Friday.

My family and I belong to the largest branch of Islam – it is known as Sunni Islam. We believe in life after death, and that the prophets are Allah's way of communicating with us. We also believe what the holy books tell us. I read the Islamic holy book, the Qur'an, every day. It makes me feel closer to Allah and helps me understand him better.

I enjoy being a Muslim. I can talk about and share my faith with other Muslims. I do find some ideas difficult to accept and have talked to my parents about them. For example, I believe that Allah is powerful and controls everything. This means that he knows us, including me, very well. I do find it difficult, however, to understand therefore how I have free will. If Allah knows what I am going to do and controls this, am I actually free to make my own choices? To help me understand some of the beliefs of Islam better, I have read parts of the Qur'an and looked to the example of the Prophet Muhammad. They help me to understand my faith better and realise how important it is for me to lead a good life as Allah intended.

I know that other Muslims may hold different beliefs from me or interpret their faith in a different way. I also know that there are other religions in the world. I have shared a few ideas of mine with you. If you have any questions, ask me in your reply and I will try to explain them to you. It would also be great to know more about you and your religious beliefs if you have any.

I look forward to hearing from you.

Rayan

Figure 1.10 The Qur'an

Activities ?

1   What key Islamic beliefs does Rayan mention in his email?

2   What Islamic key words does he use in his email? Can you explain what each one means?

3   What Muslim beliefs does Rayan mention where he has not used the Islamic term? Can you say what term he could have used?

4   How important do you think Islam is to Rayan and why do you think this?

5   Do you think Rayan finds it easy to be a Muslim? Why or why not?

6   Write a reply to Rayan, asking him questions about his faith. Include your own ideas and beliefs about religion to share your thoughts.

7   Consider what Rayan has said in his email to help you plan responses to the following statements. Make sure you include arguments that both agree and disagree with the statement.
    a   'Tawhid is the most important belief in Islam.'
    b   'Islam is a way of life that affects all aspects of a Muslim's life.'
    c   'Religion is more important today than it has ever been before.'

8   Once you have planned your arguments, debate them in a group to see who can offer the strongest response.

Exam tip

• Make sure that when you offer arguments to support a point of view, you include examples to help you.

• Structure your arguments in a logical and organised way. Make sure you consider what arguments may be given in response, so you can prepare an answer.

• Make sure you always use the appropriate key terms in your written and oral responses. This will show you have a good understanding of them and can use them accurately and appropriately.

Can you remember?

• Why are beliefs so important to Muslims?

• What do Muslims believe about Allah?

• Why are holy books important to Muslims?

• What roles were angels and prophets given by Allah?

• What is the link between the ideas of judgement, al-Qadr and free will?

• What do Muslims believe about life after death?

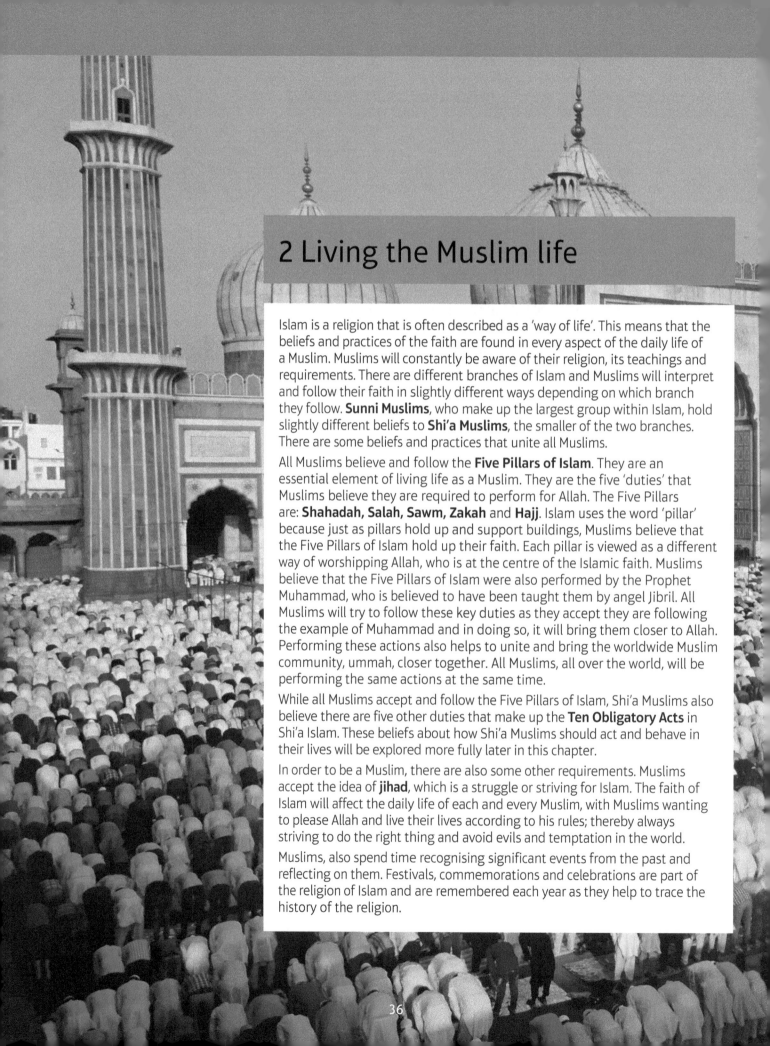

2 Living the Muslim life

Islam is a religion that is often described as a 'way of life'. This means that the beliefs and practices of the faith are found in every aspect of the daily life of a Muslim. Muslims will constantly be aware of their religion, its teachings and requirements. There are different branches of Islam and Muslims will interpret and follow their faith in slightly different ways depending on which branch they follow. **Sunni Muslims**, who make up the largest group within Islam, hold slightly different beliefs to **Shi'a Muslims**, the smaller of the two branches. There are some beliefs and practices that unite all Muslims.

All Muslims believe and follow the **Five Pillars of Islam**. They are an essential element of living life as a Muslim. They are the five 'duties' that Muslims believe they are required to perform for Allah. The Five Pillars are: **Shahadah, Salah, Sawm, Zakah** and **Hajj**. Islam uses the word 'pillar' because just as pillars hold up and support buildings, Muslims believe that the Five Pillars of Islam hold up their faith. Each pillar is viewed as a different way of worshipping Allah, who is at the centre of the Islamic faith. Muslims believe that the Five Pillars of Islam were also performed by the Prophet Muhammad, who is believed to have been taught them by angel Jibril. All Muslims will try to follow these key duties as they accept they are following the example of Muhammad and in doing so, it will bring them closer to Allah. Performing these actions also helps to unite and bring the worldwide Muslim community, ummah, closer together. All Muslims, all over the world, will be performing the same actions at the same time.

While all Muslims accept and follow the Five Pillars of Islam, Shi'a Muslims also believe there are five other duties that make up the **Ten Obligatory Acts** in Shi'a Islam. These beliefs about how Shi'a Muslims should act and behave in their lives will be explored more fully later in this chapter.

In order to be a Muslim, there are also some other requirements. Muslims accept the idea of **jihad**, which is a struggle or striving for Islam. The faith of Islam will affect the daily life of each and every Muslim, with Muslims wanting to please Allah and live their lives according to his rules; thereby always striving to do the right thing and avoid evils and temptation in the world.

Muslims, also spend time recognising significant events from the past and reflecting on them. Festivals, commemorations and celebrations are part of the religion of Islam and are remembered each year as they help to trace the history of the religion.

Learning objectives

In this chapter you will find out about:

- the Ten Obligatory Acts of Shi'a Islam
- Shahadah, the first Pillar of Islam
- Salah, the second Pillar of Islam
- Sawm, the third Pillar of Islam
- Zakah, the fourth Pillar of Islam
- Hajj, the fifth Pillar of Islam
- jihad
- Islamic festivals and celebrations.

Checkpoint

Recall

Before starting this chapter, you should remember:

- Islam is a global religion and has followers all over the world
- there are two main branches, or denominations, within Islam: Sunnis and Shi'as. They hold and interpret their beliefs slightly differently
- Muhammad is the main prophet in Islam and Muslims want to follow his example in their lives
- beliefs and actions are equally important in Islam.

Look ahead

In future chapters you will find out about:

- Islamic beliefs and attitudes towards crime and punishment
- Islamic beliefs and attitudes towards peace and conflict.

2.1 Ten Obligatory Acts of Shi'a Islam

Learning objectives

- To understand the nature, history and purpose of the Ten Obligatory Acts for Shi'a Muslims.
- To explore how they are practised by Shi'a Muslims today.
- To identify why the Ten Obligatory Acts are important for Shi'a Muslims today.

The history and nature of the Ten Obligatory Acts

An obligation is an act or a course of action that is a duty or a commitment; it is something we feel morally bound to do. The Ten Obligatory Acts, as the name suggests, are ten practices that Shi'a Muslims believe they have a duty to perform for Allah. All of the practices centre around how Muslims should live their lives and what they should do in order to worship Allah and show commitment to him.

The Ten Obligatory Acts were given by the 'Twelver' who Shi'a Muslims believe were 12 **divinely ordained** leaders, meaning they were chosen by God to become a leader; they are also known as 'the Twelve Imams'. Shi'a Muslims believe the Twelve Imams were the political and spiritual successors to Muhammad after his death. This contrasts with Sunni Muslims who accept a different line of succession from Muhammad, showing a division between the branches of Islam. Sunni Muslims believe that after Muhammad's death, it was his close companion, Abu Bakr, who was accepted by the Islamic community to follow the line of succession. The Ten Obligatory Acts were identified as the foundations of Islam for Shi'a Muslims. They include practices that involve how Muslims should live their lives, prayer, concern for others, self-purification and pilgrimage.

Shi'a Muslims believe that Allah chose Ali ibn Abi Talib, Muhammad's cousin and son-in-law, to be the correct successor after Muhammad's death. Shi'a Islam has always been the minority branch within Islam. Shi'as differ from Sunnis through their ideas on leadership, their understanding and interpretation of holy books and in some ritual practices. For example, Shi'a Muslims accept the beliefs of the Five Pillars and add the remaining obligatory practices explained here, but they combine the five compulsory prayers of Salah into three sessions in a day.

The Ten Obligatory Acts include four actions that are part of the Five Pillars of Islam, which are accepted by all Muslims, including both Sunnis and Shi'as. Although Sunnis and Shi'as both accept and recognise the essential details of these ideas, they do not refer to them by the same name or understand them in the same way.

- **Shahadah** – the first Pillar is Shahadah, which is the Declaration of Faith. This is also accepted by Shi'a Muslims, although it is not one of the Ten Obligatory Acts since it is seen throughout all of them. The Ten Obligatory Acts are:
- **Salah** – this second Pillar means performing the five daily prayers every day, although some Shi'a Muslims will combine two of the prayers, meaning they will only pray three times a day. Muslims will purify themselves prior to prayer – a process called **wudu**.

- **Zakah** – this third Pillar means each Muslim donating 2.5 per cent of their annual wealth to the poor. This will be collected by the mosque and used to help those who may be struggling.
- **Sawm** – this fourth Pillar means fasting (not eating any food or drinking any water) during the daylight hours during the month of Ramadan, the ninth month of the Islamic calendar.
- **Hajj** – this fifth Pillar means every Muslim, if physically able and financially stable, should make a pilgrimage to the holy city of Makkah once in their lifetime.

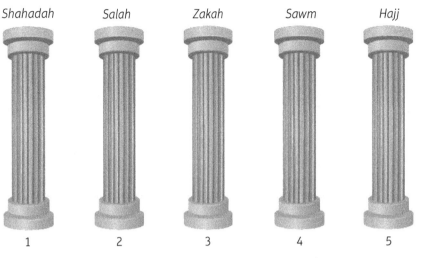

Shahadah   *Salah*   *Zakah*   *Sawm*   *Hajj*

1   2   3   4   5

Figure 2.1 Five Pillars of Islam

- **Khums** – this literally means 'fifth' and refers historically to the religious obligation of Muslims in the army to pay one-fifth of the spoils of war. This money is given to the descendants of Muhammad and Shi'a Muslims but will also be used to help the poor and needy and the Islamic clergy. This money will be collected by the state of an Islamic country or the mosque. Today it is also considered by Shi'a Muslims to include profit made and any gain from minerals or buried treasure.
- **Jihad** – this is a term that literally translates as the idea of 'to struggle'. It is generally accepted to be a struggle for Allah. It can be broken down into different types, including defending an individual, holy war and as personal daily struggles to resist temptations, like not drinking alcohol or being tempted not to spend sufficient time in prayer.
- **Amr-bil-Maroof** – commanding what is good. This is taken to mean a commandment from the Qur'an that tells Shi'a Muslims to do what is good. This would be achieved through following the rules from the Qur'an and Hadith. It may include how they should act towards others or following how Allah has commanded them to live their lives.
- **Nahi Anil Munkar** – forbid what is evil. This means that Muslims need to resist temptation and they should not commit sins against Allah. This could include things such as lapsing from following the Five Pillars of Islam.
- **Tawalla** – expressing love towards good. This is the idea of showing love towards the prophets of Allah and those who stand up for truth and justice. This could be in the way Muslims follow the examples of the prophets in their lives or how they support other Muslims who stand up against injustices in the world.
- **Tabarra** – moving away from evil. This is taken to mean staying away from those who are viewed as evil oppressors, those who choose to turn away from Allah and those who are enemies of Islam. If a person chooses to not accept Allah in their lives, it is best for other Muslims to stay away from them in case they too are tempted to turn away from Allah.

Sources of authority

Some of the Ten Obligatory Acts are referenced in the Qur'an:

The Believers, men and women, are protectors one of another: they enjoin what is just, and forbid what is evil: they observe regular prayers, practise regular charity, and obey Allah and His Messenger. On them will Allah pour His mercy: for Allah is Exalted in power, Wise. Allah has promised to Believers, men and women, Gardens under which rivers flow, to dwell therein, and beautiful mansions in Gardens of everlasting bliss. But the greatest bliss is the good pleasure of Allah: that is the supreme felicity. O Prophet! strive hard against the Unbelievers and the Hypocrites, and be firm against them. Their abode is Hell,—an evil refuge indeed. (Surah 9:71–73)

The purpose of the Ten Obligatory Acts

The purpose of the Ten Obligatory Acts for Shi'a Muslims is to:

- identify the key Shi'a Islamic beliefs that form the foundation of their religion
- allow Shi'a Muslims to worship Allah through their beliefs and actions
- bring them closer to Allah and follow his rules and laws.

Figure 2.2 Allah drawn in Arabic

Why are the Ten Obligatory Acts important for Shi'a Muslims today?

The Ten Obligatory Acts today unite Shi'a Muslims and are important in bringing them together. It gives purpose to their lives and helps them to understand how they should behave on a daily basis. Muslims will face challenges from modern society and the Acts help them to identify in their daily lives how they should act and how Allah wants them to live their lives.

Exam-style questions

Outline three features of the Ten Obligatory Acts for Shi'a Muslims. **(3 marks)**

Exam tip

This question requires you to identify three things about the Ten Obligatory Acts. Remember that Shi'a Muslims follow all ten of the practices and some of them make up the Five Pillars of Islam. Be careful to be clear in your answer and do not mix up ideas.

Activities

1. Explain what obligatory acts you have to perform in your life. Think about the things you do as a ritual at regular points in your life. Explain why they are important to you.
2. Read through each of the Ten Obligatory Acts explained above. Explain who you think benefits from each one and why.
3. In pairs, discuss the following statement: 'It would be difficult to follow all Ten Obligatory Acts.' Create a table showing any arguments you can think of to agree with the statement and any arguments that you think disagree with it.

Extend your knowledge

The Ten Obligatory Acts are also known as the Ten Ancillaries of Faith for Shi'a Muslims. Shi'as use this term because an ancillary is something that provides support. In this case, the Ten Ancillaries of Faith for Shi'a Muslims are the ten practices and beliefs that support everything that happens within the religion.

Summary

- The Ten Obligatory Acts are ten practices that Shi'a Muslims believe are duties they have to perform.
- Four of the Ten Obligatory Acts also make up four of the Five Pillars of Islam, which all Muslims, including Sunnis and Shi'as, accept.
- Shi'a Muslims believe the Ten Obligatory Acts help them to get closer to Allah and live their lives as he intended.

Checkpoint

Strengthen

S1 Which branch of Islam accepts the Ten Obligatory Acts?

S2 Which of the Ten Obligatory Acts are also found in the Five Pillars of Islam?

S3 Name and explain each of the Ten Obligatory Acts.

Challenge

C1 Why do you think Shahadah, the Declaration of Faith in Allah and Muhammad, is not one of the Ten Obligatory Acts?

C2 How important do you think the Ten Obligatory Acts are to Shi'a Muslims? Explain your answer.

C3 Which of the Ten Obligatory Acts do you think Shi'a Muslims find most difficult to perform and why?

2.2 Shahadah as one of the Five Pillars

Learning objectives

- To understand the nature and role of Shahadah for Sunni and Shi'a Muslims.
- To recognise the significance of Shahadah for all Muslims.
- To explore why reciting the Shahadah is important for Muslims and its place in Muslim practices today.

Shahadah, the first Pillar of Islam

The first Pillar of Islam is Shahadah and is the Declaration of Faith. It is where Muslims state their belief in one god who is Allah, and in the Prophet Muhammad. Muslims believe that they should submit to Allah in all aspects of their life. This means that they should accept that Allah is a supreme being who is greater than them in all aspects of their lives. They demonstrate this through the way they behave and act, and this can be seen within the Five Pillars. The Shahadah is a statement that Muslims will repeat, showing that they recognise the power and supremacy of Allah in their lives, as well as the prominence given to Muhammad as the Prophet chosen by Allah.

The Shahadah contains two of the key beliefs of Islam that sum up what it means to be a Muslim:

- to believe in one god called Allah. This is Tawhid and is central to Islam.
- to confirm they accept Muhammad as the prophet of Allah.

Shahadah

Declaration of Faith

Figure 2.3 Shahadah, the first Pillar of Islam

Sources of authority

The Shahadah, the Declaration of Faith

La ilaha illallah muhammadur rasulullah (There is no god but Allah and Muhammad is the Messenger of Allah.)

The Qur'an reinforces the importance of the Shahadah for Muslims when it says:

There is no god but He: that is the witness of Allah, His angels, and those endued with knowledge, standing firm on justice. There is no god but He, the Exalted in Power, the Wise. (Surah 3:18)

Reciting the Shahadah

Muslims accept that it is important to recite the Shahadah out loud. It is considered to be essential to say out loud the central ideas of the faith since it confirms, both to the person speaking and those listening, that the person is claiming to be a Muslim. It will be spoken the first time a person formally declares that they are a Muslim and should at this time be stated three times in front of witnesses. A Muslim is expected to speak these words out loud with sincerity and the full understanding of what they mean.

The Shahadah makes up part of the **adhan** or the call to prayer, which is given five times a day from the mosque. This tells Muslims that it is time to pray and Muslims will try to go to the mosque to take part in the prayers communally. The adhan is also spoken into the ears of newborn babies and, if possible, is spoken as the final words just before death. It is believed to be important for these words to be the first and last words that a Muslim hears, because as a Muslim it would be the first and last thing they are aware of in their lives.

Muslims will also teach the Shahadah to children and repeat it throughout the day at other times when they are not praying. They believe that their

Figure 2.4 Whispering the adhan into the ear of a newborn baby

submission to the one god, Allah, is so important to them that they need to be aware of it all the time and show it outwardly all the time. As a Declaration of Faith, reciting the Shahadah is one of the simplest ways of doing this, and they believe that it will be rewarded by Allah.

Sources of authority

The adhan

Allah is the Greatest (say three times)

I bear witness that there is no god but Allah (say twice)

I bear witness that Muhammad is Allah's messenger (say twice)

Rush to prayer (say twice)

Rush to success (say twice)

Allah is the Greatest (say twice)

There is no god but Allah

Why is the Shahadah important to all Muslims?

The Shahadah is fundamental to a Muslim's way of life for a number of reasons.

- It contains the basic beliefs of Islam, which are central to the faith. These are belief in Tawhid, the ideas of one god and in the Prophet Muhammad.

- It is seen to be the starting point of Muslim beliefs. When the Shahadah is stated, it is accepted that a person is showing their commitment to following Islam and submitting to Allah throughout their life. By repeating the Shahadah regularly, a Muslim shows that their commitment to Allah is continuous – they are constantly renewing it.

- It reinforces beliefs in Tawhid and Risalah, which are contained in the Six Beliefs of Islam.

- Muslims believe their whole life should be lived in submission to Allah and that stating the Declaration of Faith demonstrates this.

- The first Pillar underpins and supports the other Pillars as they are further acts of showing submission to Allah.

- All Muslims believe in the Shahadah, showing they are united as a community or ummah. The Shahadah can be spoken to another person and with a group of people, so it strengthens a person's identity as part of the Islamic faith.

Activities

1. If you had to write one statement that summed up your beliefs about life, what would you write? Share your ideas with your partner. Were your thoughts the same or different? Why? As an extension, explain why it doesn't matter if your thoughts are different to other people.

2. Complete the following sentence by making a list which explains the importance of Shahadah: 'The First Pillar of Islam, Shahadah, helps Muslims to…'

3. Imagine a Muslim has just spoken the Shahadah for the first time. How do you think they would feel? Why? What differences or changes do you think it might make to their life? Complete a written piece of work that explains your thoughts.

Can you remember?

- What are the Six Beliefs of Islam for Sunni Muslims and which ones are related to Shahadah?
- Why is Muhammad so important to Muslims?
- Why are the Five Pillars of Islam considered to be important for every Muslim to perform?

Exam-style question

Outline two reasons why the Shahadah is important to Muslims. **(3 marks)**

Exam tip

The examiner requires you to give two different reasons to answer this question successfully. You need to STATE the reason and the DEVELOP it to achieve the full four marks available.

Sources of authority

Those who show patience, firmness and self-control; who are true (in word and deed); who worship devoutly; who spend (in the way of Allah); and who pray for forgiveness in the early hours of the morning. There is no god but He: that is the witness of Allah, His angels, and those endued with knowledge, standing firm on justice. There is no god but He, the Exalted in Power, the Wise. The Religion before Allah is Islam (submission to His Will): nor did the People of the Book dissent therefrom except through envy of each other, after knowledge had come to them. But if any deny the Signs of Allah, Allah is swift in calling to account. So if they dispute with you, say: "I have submitted my whole self to Allah and so have those who follow me." And say to the People of the Book and to those who are unlearned: "Do you (also) submit yourselves?" If they do, they are in right guidance, but if they turn back, your duty is to convey the Message; and in Allah's sight are (all) His servants. As to those who deny the Signs of Allah and in defiance of right, slay the prophets, and slay those who teach just dealing with mankind, announce to them a grievous penalty. (Surah 3:17-21)

Summary

- The Five Pillars of Islam are the basic duties that every Muslim should perform.
- Shahadah is the Declaration of Faith and is the first Pillar of Islam.
- The Shahadah is also part of the adhan – the call to prayer.
- Muslims believe the Shahadah is important as it states every Muslim's belief in Tawhid, the belief in one god and belief in Muhammad, the Prophet or Messenger of Allah.

Checkpoint

Strengthen

S1 Which of the Five Pillars is Shahadah?

S2 What two important Muslim beliefs does the Shahadah contain and what are their Islamic names?

S3 When should the words of the Shahadah be spoken by Muslims?

Challenge

C1 Why do you think the Shahadah should be recited three times in front of witnesses?

C2 What do you think happens if a person is unable to say the Shahadah for themselves prior to death?

C3 How does reciting the Shahadah show submission to Allah for Muslims?

2.3 Salah as one of the Five Pillars

Learning objectives

- To understand the nature, history, significance and purpose of Salah for Sunni and Shi'a Muslims.
- To explore how Salah is performed.
- To identify and understand prayer in the mosque, home and the Jummah service.

Sources of authority

But celebrate the praises of your Lord, and be of those who prostrate themselves in adoration. And serve your Lord until there come unto you the Hour that is certain (death). (Surah 15:98–99)

Recite what is sent of the Book by inspiration to you, and establish regular Prayer: for Prayer restrains from shameful and unjust deeds; and remembrance of Allah is the greatest (thing in life) without doubt. And Allah knows the (deeds) that you do. (Surah 29:45)

Sources of authority

So (give) glory to Allah, when you reach eventide and when you rise in the morning. Indeed, to Him be praise, in the heavens and on earth; and in the late afternoon and when the day begins to decline. (Surah 30:17–18)

… and celebrate (constantly) the praises of your Lord before the rising of the sun, and before its setting; indeed, celebrate them for part of the hours of the night, and at the sides of the day… (Surah 20:130)

Islamic beliefs about Salah

The second Pillar of Islam is called Salah and is compulsory prayer. Reference to Sunni and Shi'a Muslims recognising that regular prayer is a requirement in Islam as it is a requirement and seen to be a way of getting guidance from Allah. Muslims see prayer as communication with Allah and believe that this should take place regularly. Allah gave rules about prayer to the angel Jibril, who gave them to the Prophet Muhammad. They are also contained in the Qur'an. Muslims believe that through prayer they can get closer to Allah and understand him better. It also reflects submission to Allah, one of the key ideas in Islam.

Salah

Figure 2.5 Salah, the second Pillar of Islam

Although both Sunni and Shi'a Muslims recognise the importance of Salah, they may give it differing levels of significance. Sunni Muslims consider those who do not pray five times a day unbelievers, whereas Shi'a Muslims may practise the act of Salah differently and therefore give emphasis to different methods. They differ in their practice of the Pillar of Salah. Salah takes place at set times, five times a day. Sunni Muslims follow this, but Shi'a Muslims combine two of the Salahs, and pray only three times a day. Sunni Muslims also touch their foreheads directly to the floor as part of the practise of prayer, but Shi'a Muslims rest their heads on a plank of wood.

These verses from the Qur'an give Muslims the five times of prayer for Salah. They are related to the sun and change with the seasons, occurring at different times of the day throughout the year. They are:

1 **Fajr** – morning prayer (between dawn and sunrise)
2 **Zuhr** – midday prayer
3 **Asr** – late afternoon prayer
4 **Maghrib** – sunset prayer
5 **Isha** – night prayer.

Preparing for prayer

When it is time for Muslims to pray, the **muezzin**, or crier, gives the adhan from the **minaret**, the tower on a mosque. This is a call to prayer and incorporates the Declaration of Faith, the Shahadah. All Muslims will try to attend the prayers.

Before Muslims pray, they must wash themselves in a practice called wudu to ensure they are physically and spiritually clean and ready. This is to show respect to Allah and to make sure they are in the correct frame of mind to concentrate on their prayers to Allah. They wash the exposed parts of the body and those that are used during the prayers (**Figure 2.6**).

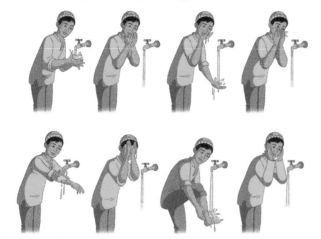

Figure 2.6 The practice of wudu that takes place before prayer

Performing Salah

The Ka'bah is the sacred shrine in Makkah that is the main focal point in the fifth Pillar of Islam, Hajj or pilgrimage. The Ka'bah is believed to be the first house of worship, which Allah instructed the prophets Ibrahim and Isma'il to build. It is in modern-day Saudi Arabia, and many Muslims will travel to visit and worship it. Muslims believe that it is important to pray towards the Ka'bah at all times, even if they are far away in different countries. The direction of Makkah and the Ka'bah is indicated in mosques by the **mihrab**, which is an alcove in the **qiblah** wall. The qiblah wall is at the front of the mosque and all Muslims face it when praying. If Muslims are not in the mosque, they use a compass to find the correct direction to face. For Muslims in Britain this is roughly towards the south east.

In the mosque

Muslims stand in rows, shoulder to shoulder, to pray. This is to show equality and solidarity. Salah consists of set words that are said by the imam, or prayer leader, when Muslims are in the mosque. All Muslim men are expected to attend the mosque on Friday, which is the Islamic holy day. This service is known as the Jummah prayer and is when Muslims come together as a community to pray. It takes place just after noon and replaces the zuhr prayer. During this service, the imam gives a sermon about a current issue in the world and Muslims join together to form the ummah.

Women do not have to attend the mosque, although some choose to do so. They pray in a separate section of the mosque to the part used by men. Muslims believe that when praying there should be no distractions by other people and Muslims should not concentrate on anything except Allah.

When Muslims pray, they follow a set system of movements called **rakahs**. These can be described as standing, bowing and lying down prostrating. Sunni Muslims fold their arms as part of this practice, whereas Shi'a Muslims do not. The rakahs demonstrate ideas of obedience and submission to Allah because Muslims are lowering themselves below Allah. This action reflects the idea of Muslims dedicating themselves to Allah in every aspect of their lives.

Figure 2.7 The rakahs that Muslims follow during prayers. Muslims are not expected to attend the Mosque five times a day. Islam recognises that Muslims are able to pray anywhere that is clean. Often this can take place at home, which means they can worship with other members of the family. Many places of work or schools provide a room where Muslims can pray.

Why is prayer important for Muslims?

Prayer is important because:

- it is regular communication with Allah
- it helps Muslims to connect to Allah and to remember that their lives should be in submission to Allah
- it is one of the Five Pillars of Islam and therefore is a duty that every Muslim should perform
- Salah offers time for Muslims to step away from daily life and reflect on their faith. It allows them to focus on Allah, which is the purpose of their existence. Muslims will often follow the set prayers of Salah with a **du'a** or prayer of the heart, which is a personal prayer to Allah.

It is also important that the prayers are said with the right intention – Muslims believe that just saying the prayers is meaningless if they do not feel and understand the words, and they must truly submit to Allah for the prayers to benefit them.

Similarities and differences between Muslims and Christians

Prayer is important in both Islam and Christianity as a regular form of communication with God. Both have set prayers which they may complete either as part of a service or individually. They also both have the flexibility to worship in their holy buildings or at home. However, there are fundamental differences between Muslims and Christians regarding prayer, as follows.

- Muslims perform the rakahs whilst praying, whereas Christians tend to stay in one position, possibly with their hands together.
- Muslims face Makkah – their holy city – whilst praying.
- Muslims and Christians both believe in one god but Christians may direct their prayers towards the idea of the Trinity. This is their belief that God is understood in three ways (the Father, Son and Holy Spirit) which Muslims do not understand or accept.
- Although Christians may have common times to pray, they are flexible whereas Muslims have fixed times to pray throughout the day.
- Before prayer, Muslims perform wudu, their ritual washing, whereas Christians do not.

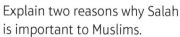

Activities ?

1. Imagine you have been asked to explain Salah to a group of non-Muslims. Write ten bullet points explaining what you feel are the most important pieces of information they need to know.

2. Consider this statement: 'Prayer is a waste of time.' Write a paragraph offering arguments for what a Muslim would say about this statement. Then write a paragraph explaining your own view. Share your thoughts with a partner.

Sources of authority

… for Prayer restrains from shameful and unjust deeds… And Allah knows the (deeds) that you do. (Surah 29:45)

Exam-style question

Explain two reasons why Salah is important to Muslims.

(4 marks)

Exam tip

There is a lot of information about Salah, so think about this question carefully. It is not asking you what happens when Muslims perform Salah but instead why it is important for Muslims to perform Salah. Think carefully about your answer before you write it and make sure you develop each reason fully, giving detail for each idea.

Summary

- Salah is the second Pillar of Islam and means compulsory prayer five times every day.
- The times for prayer are set, but change with the seasons throughout the year.
- Muslims face the Ka'bah in Makkah when they pray and stand shoulder to shoulder.
- Muslim men are expected to attend the Jummah service at the mosque on a Friday.
- Muslims can pray anywhere that is clean.
- Muslims have to perform wudu, which is washing exposed parts of the body, such as the face and hands, before prayer.
- Muslims perform rakahs, a set series of movements, when they pray.

Checkpoint

Strengthen

S1 Where do the rules about prayer for Muslims come from?
S2 How do Muslims make sure they are ready to pray?
S3 Why is prayer so important to Muslims?

Challenge

C1 How does standing shoulder to shoulder in prayer demonstrate ideas of equality and solidarity in Islam?
C2 How do the rakahs, the prayer positions of standing, bowing and prostrating, demonstrate submission to Allah?
C3 Why do you think Muslims are expected to attend the Jummah service?

2.4 Sawm as one of the Five Pillars

Learning objectives

- To understand the nature, role, significance and purpose of fasting during Ramadan.
- To explore who is excused from fasting and why.
- To understand the nature, history, significance and purpose of the Night of Power.
- To identify why Laylat al-Qadr is important for Muslims today.

Fasting

Sawm is the fourth pillar of Islam and means fasting. All Muslims must fast and Sawm happens during the ninth month of the Islam calendar, called **Ramadan**. For the whole month of Ramadan, every healthy adult Muslim should go without food and drink during daylight hours and should not indulge in anything considered to be sinful, such as offending another person, or having bad thoughts about others.

Sawm

Fasting

Figure 2.8 Sawm, the fourth Pillar of Islam

The month of Ramadan is very important to Muslims because it was during this month that Muhammad received his first revelation of the Qur'an. Fasting is performed as part of the commemoration of this event and is detailed in the Qur'an, Surah 2:183–185.

What are the rules of fasting?

Muslims are very strict about fasting and believe that nothing should pass the lips. This includes food, drink (including water), chewing gum or smoke from cigarettes. It can take a lot of self-discipline to follow the rules of fasting. Muslims also believe that during the month of Ramadan they should resist the urge to be involved in any idle chatter or unkind words about anyone else. Muslims believe that unintentional eating or drinking, for example, swallowing water when showering, is an accident and does not cancel the fast.

Muslims follow a **lunar calendar**, which is based on the moon cycles. This means that the Islamic months do not run at the same time each year because each month starts with a new moon. This means that the month of Ramadan moves throughout the year. This can mean that sometimes Ramadan can take place in the summer and in other years it can take place in the winter.

Who should fast?

Muslims believe that every healthy adult who is able should take part in fasting during Ramadan. Children from around the age of 10 will usually take part in Ramadan, as they are considered to be old enough to understand the significance of the act. There is a need to be healthy to ensure that fasting does not cause any serious threat to health. This means that some people are excused from fasting. These include women who are menstruating, pregnant or breastfeeding. Other groups who are excused include those who are sick or who might harm themselves by fasting.

If a Muslim is in the army or tackling a long journey, they are also excused from the fast because they need their energy to keep up their strength. The elderly are another group of Muslims who are excused, as well as young children.

If a person cannot fast, either for the entire month of Ramadan or just for a short period within Ramadan, they are advised to make up any missed days at another time. If they cannot do this, they are required to give the cost of two meals to the poor for each day they miss.

What is the significance and purpose of fasting?

- The Qur'an says that Sawm is an obligatory duty for Muslims to perform as it is one of the Five Pillars.
- Muslims believe that fasting helps them to appreciate everything that Allah has provided for them.
- Having to give up something teaches Muslims self-control and discipline as they need to overcome the challenge of going without food and water in the daylight hours.

Sources of authority

O you who believe! Fasting is prescribed to you as it was prescribed to those before you, that you may (learn) self-restraint – (Surah 2:183)

- The Prophet Muhammad himself is believed to have fasted when he was alive and he gave the instruction of following Sawm in his final sermon.
- Muslims believe experiencing the hardship of not eating and drinking will also teach them how the poor and needy suffer. This will teach them the idea of compassion and help them try to be less greedy and selfish in their own lives.

Muslims also believe that fasting has rewards for them. The first reward is the celebration of breaking the fast at the end of Ramadan, where they might share a meal with friends and family. This is also recognised in the formal celebration of the festival of **Id-ul-Fitr** where they will celebrate the end of the month of Ramadan and the fast. The second reward will be in the afterlife on the Day of Judgement, as Muslims believe they will be judged by Allah for the way they have acted in their lives on Earth once the world ends and this will determine whether they are rewarded in al-Jannah, Paradise, or punished in Jahannam, Hell.

Laylat al-Qadr: Night of Power

Laylat al-Qadr is the occasion celebrated today to remember when Muhammad first received the revelations of the Qur'an. It is believed that this occurred during the final period of the month of Ramadan. Muhammad was in a cave on Mount Hira, spending quiet time in meditation and reflection when this event occurred. He claimed to have had a religious experience where a vision appeared and commanded him to recite (read). Later this vision was identified as the Archangel Jibril. Since Muhammad could not read, he protested that he was unable to do this. Eventually he realised that he was being commanded to recite and speak what he was told. In this way, the Qur'an was revealed to him.

Figure 2.9 A card to celebrate Ramadan

Why is Laylat al-Qadr significant for Muslims today?

It is important for several reasons.

- It is through this event that Muhammad realised he had been chosen to be a prophet of Allah.
- It is singled out as a time for celebration because it was through this event that the Qur'an was revealed.
- It is a time to mark and remember the arrival of the final guidance from Allah to humanity. Muslims believe it is the final, perfect version of Allah's words.
- Some Muslims believe it to be the holiest night of the year and a time to receive special blessings. For this reason, many Muslims will offer special prayers known as du'a during this time.

Activities

1 How difficult do you think a Muslim living in Britain would find performing the Pillar of Sawm? Explain at least three reasons to support your answer. Do you think a Muslim living in a hot country might face different issues? Why or why not?

2 Sawm is completed for a number of different reasons, including self-control and discipline. Make a list of things in your life that encourage this idea. Explain how.

Exam-style question

Explain two features of the Pillar of Sawm. **(4 marks)**

Exam tip

You need to demonstrate your knowledge and understanding of the Pillar of Sawm in this answer. Identify two different features of Sawm and develop each idea fully by explaining what you know about it. Try to give examples to expand on the points you make.

Can you remember?

- Why is Muhammad so important within the religion of Islam?
- What happened to Muhammad on the Night of Power?
- Why are the Five Pillars of Islam so important to Muslims and what differences are there in the practices of Sunni and Shi'a Muslims?

Summary

- Sawm is the fourth Pillar of Islam.
- Sawm means Muslims should fast by not eating or drinking and by giving up pleasures in daylight hours during the ninth month, called Ramadan.
- The elderly, children, those going on journeys and some women are exempt from fasting.
- Fasting is performed as a duty since it is a Pillar. It teaches self-discipline and helps to give an understanding of how the poor can suffer.
- Laylat al-Qadr is the Night of Power, when Muhammad was first believed to have had the Qur'an revealed to him.
- As the Night of Power is believed to have happened during the month of Ramadan, it is a special time for Muslims to remember.

Checkpoint

Strengthen

S1 Which Pillar is Sawm and when does it take place?

S2 Who is exempt from fasting and why?

S3 What is Laylat al-Qadr?

Challenge

C1 When in the year do you think it would be hardest to fast and why?

C2 What do you think is the most important reason why Muslims fast and why?

C3 Why do you think many Muslims may spend extra time in prayer and reading the Qur'an during the month of Ramadan?

2.5 Zakah as one of the Five Pillars, and Khums

Learning objectives

- To understand the nature, role, significance and purpose of Zakah and Khums.
- To explore why Zakah is important for Sunni Muslims and Khums is important for Shi'a Muslims.
- To consider the benefits of Zakah and Khums.

Zakah

Figure 2.10 Zakah, the third Pillar of Islam

Figure 2.11 Payment of Zakah

Zakah

Zakah is the third Pillar of Islam and is an obligatory poor tax. It is often translated to mean 'charity', 'alms', 'welfare' or 'tax'. It is a type of charity that is intended to help the poor. It was first instituted by Abu Bakr, who Sunni Muslims believe to be the Prophet Muhammad's successor. All Muslims are expected to perform Zakah once a year and this involves giving 2.5 per cent of their wealth to the needy and the ummah. The money they give is what they can afford after they have taken care of their family's needs, so it may include savings or extra money they have earned within a year. A Muslim will also only pay Zakah if their wealth is above a certain minimum amount – this is known as **nisab**.

Muslims believe that everything, including money, has been given to them from Allah. They believe that they do not own it but they are looking after it for Allah. Zakah is part of this and therefore it is not to be seen as a negative tax to be avoided. Instead, it is a way for Muslims to purify themselves, to try to make themselves less selfish and greedy. It prevents Muslims from becoming too reliant on money and teaches them the importance of sharing with others.

Zakah is seen as a form of worship because the money is given in the name of Allah. It demonstrates the idea of submission to Allah as the pillar is not seen as optional, but as a duty they must perform. It is also seen as a good thing as it is the ummah that benefits from it. The Muslims who receive Zakah also see it as a form of purification, as they are taught ideas of gratefulness rather than envy. Zakah is usually received as money but it can be received as food and goods. Sometimes it may also be received as support for educational needs.

The Qur'an talks about Zakah in Surah 9:58–60, and sets out the groups of people who should receive Zakah.

Sources of authority

Alms are for the poor and the needy, and those employed to administer the (funds); for those whose hearts have been (recently) reconciled (to Truth); for those in bondage and in debt; in the cause of Allah; and for the wayfarer: (thus is it) ordained by Allah and Allah is full of knowledge and wisdom.
(Surah 9:60)

According to Islamic law, Muslim countries have the authority to collect and distribute Zakah. Some Muslim states follow this practice, while others and many non-Muslim countries leave it to the individual Muslim to organise their payment. In the UK, the money is often collected by the local mosque for distribution. Failure to pay Zakah is taken by Muslims as a sign of unbelief in Allah and the religion of Islam. There have also been legal arguments in the Islamic community about what action to take if a Muslim fails to pay, such as suggestions to take it forcibly. In countries run on Islamic law, failure to pay Zakah is viewed as similar to tax evasion.

Why is Zakah important for Sunni Muslims?

Muslims believe that Allah wants them to care for his creation. In showing generosity and care they are also showing that they acknowledge this responsibility and the greatness of Allah. Zakah is also important because:

- it is one of the Five Pillars and therefore is a duty that Muslims should perform
- it is seen as an act of worship towards Allah because they are showing care for his creations
- it teaches better-off Muslims to empathise with the poor and needy and try to put the teachings of helping others into practice
- it benefits the ummah, helping Muslims to feel that they belong and are contributing to Islam as a whole.

Khums

In the Islamic tradition, Khums refers to the historic religious obligation of Muslims in the army to pay one-fifth (20 per cent) of the spoils of war to the Caliph or Sultan. In Shi'a Islam, Khums is one of the Ten Obligatory Acts they are expected to perform. Shi'a Muslims also pay Zakah. In Shi'a understanding, Khums includes the gains of war, objects obtained from the sea, treasure, mineral resources, gainful earnings, lawful earnings that have become unlawful, and land. Traditionally, the recipients of Khums have been the descendants of Muhammad and Shi'a Islamic faith. A portion of the money is also believed to be set aside in

Shi'a Islam for the current recognised Shi'a imam, leader, and is distributed to causes on his behalf by Islamic scholars.

Zakah differs from Khums in that Zakah is used to help the poor and needy generally, whereas Khums is used to benefit solely those considered in Shi'a Islam to be the rightful descendants of Muhammad. Sunni Muslims do not view Khums in the same way as Shi'a Islam because of the differences that emerged between the two groups after the death of Muhammad.

Why is Khums important and what are the benefits of Khums?

Khums is similar to Zakah in that it demonstrates a Muslim's belief that they must be generous and care for Allah's creation. It is important for Shi'a Muslims because:

- it is a duty and is one of the Ten Obligatory Acts that Shi'as are expected to follow and perform
- it is mentioned in the Qur'an , particularly in Surah 8:1 and 8:36–42
- special recognition is given to the Prophet Muhammad and his family and this is where this money goes
- Muslims believe that wealth is the property of Allah, and so Khums teaches them to respect and look after Allah's gifts. Through the distribution of Khums, Shi'a Muslims recognise the importance of the descendants of Muhammad and Shi'a Islam, believing the rightful heirs have been identified and provision is made for them
- Khums can be used to benefit those who are needy, who are also accepted descendants of Muhammad, therefore following the traditional teachings of Islam of helping others who are less fortunate
- Khums is also used in Shi'a Islam for educational purposes and some money may be used to benefit theological schools or other things that are felt to be necessary in religious matters.

Sources of authority

They ask you concerning (things taken as) spoils of war. Say: '(Such) spoils are at the disposal of Allah and the Messenger: So fear Allah, and keep straight the relations between yourselves: obey Allah and His Prophet, if you do believe. (Surah 8:1)

And know that out of all the booty that you may acquire (in war), a fifth share is assigned to Allah – and to the Messenger, and to near relatives, orphans, the needy and the wayfarer… (Surah 8:41)

Activities ?

1 Imagine you have the following amounts of money. How much would need to be given in Zakah? How much money would need to be given in Khums? Explain what your opinion is on Muslims giving this amount of money and why.

   a £100   **b** £1,000   **c** £5,000

2 Read the first Qur'anic quote in this section that explains the groups of people that should receive Zakah. Make a list of these people. Explain why do you think these are the people identified as those who should receive this charity money?

3 Write one paragraph on Zakah and one on Khums to show how they demonstrate submission to Allah.

Exam-style question

Explain two reasons why Zakah and Khums are important in Islam. In your answer you must refer to a source of wisdom and authority. **(5 marks)**

Exam tip

Remember that Zakah is one of the five Pillars of Islam and Khums is one of the Ten Obligatory Acts. Make sure the reasons you give show why they are both important. You may also show awareness within your answer of how Sunni and Shi'a beliefs differ.

Extend your knowledge

Zakah is identified as Muslims giving 2.5 per cent of their wealth. Muslims are able to offer more if they wish and this is known as **sadaqah**. These are voluntary contributions, given at any time, to help those in need and the poor. They may be given when a natural disaster has happened. Sadaqah can also be extended to mean time, talents, prayer, sympathy or a happy smile. Any helpful deed towards a Muslim or non-Muslim could be counted as sadaqah.

Summary

- Zakah is the third pillar of Islam and means charity or tax.
- Muslims are expected to give 2.5 per cent of their residual wealth in Zakah.
- Zakah will be collected by the Islamic government or local mosque.
- Zakah is used to help the poor and needy.
- Khums is a Shi'a Muslim practice that means giving 20 per cent of certain types of income.
- There are set people who are expected to receive Khums.

Checkpoint

Strengthen

S1 Which pillar is Zakah and how much are Muslims expected to give in Zakah?

S2 What is Khums and which branch of Islam follows this teaching?

S3 Why are Zakah and Khums important?

Challenge

C1 How do you think a Muslim would feel about receiving Zakah?

C2 How are Zakah and Khums an act of worship to Allah?

2.6 Hajj as one of the Five Pillars

Learning objectives

- To understand the nature, role, origins and significance of Hajj.
- To identify how Hajj is performed and why it is important for Muslims.
- To explore the benefits and challenges of Hajj.

Hajj

Hajj, or pilgrimage, to Makkah is the fifth Pillar of Islam. It is a sacred journey that happens once a year during the month of **Dhul-Hijjah**, which is the twelfth month in the Islamic calendar. Hajj is a duty that every Muslim should try to complete once in their lifetime. However, it is physically demanding and can be expensive, so not every Muslim will be able to achieve this goal.

Origins of Hajj

Sources of authority

Our Lord! Make of us Muslims, bowing to Your (Will), and of our progeny a people Muslim, bowing to Your (Will); and show us our place for the celebration of (due) rites; and turn unto us (in Mercy); for You are the Oft-Returning, Most Merciful. Our Lord! Send amongst them a Messenger of their own, who shall rehearse Your Signs to them and instruct them in scripture and wisdom, and sanctify them: for You are the Exalted in Might, the Wise." And who turns away from the religion of Abraham but such as debase their souls with folly? Him We chose and rendered pure in this world: and he will be in the Hereafter in the ranks of the Righteous.

(Surah 2:128–130)

Hajj

Pilgrimage

Figure 2.12 Hajj, the fifth Pillar of Islam

Sources of authority

And remember that Abraham was tried by his Lord with certain Commands, which he fulfilled: He said: "I will make you an Imam to the Nations." He pleaded: "And also (Imams) from my offspring!" He answered: "But My Promise is not within the reach of evil-doers." Remember We made the House a place of assembly for men and a place of safety; and take you the station of Abraham as a place of prayer; and We covenanted with Abraham and Isma'il, that they should sanctify My House for those who compass it round, or use it as a retreat, or bow, or prostrate themselves (therein in prayer). And remember Abraham said: "My Lord, Make this a City of Peace, and feed its people with fruits,—such of them as believe in Allah and the Last Day." He said: "(Yea), and such as reject Faith,—for a while will I grant them their pleasure, but will soon drive them to the torment of Fire,—an evil destination (indeed)!" And remember Abraham and Isma'il raised the foundations of the House (with this prayer): "Our Lord! Accept (this service) from us: for You are the All-hearing, the All-knowing.

(Surah 2:124–127)

The origins of Hajj date back to the time of **Isma'il** when he and his mother, **Hagar**, were stranded in the desert. Hagar ran between the hills of Marwa and Safa looking for water until the angel Jibril created a spring of fresh water. Isma'il is the son of the **Prophet Ibrahim** and following the order of Allah, Muslims believe he built the Ka'bah, the sacred shrine, on this site in Makkah.

In 630 CE, Muslims believe Muhammad led a group of Muslims on the first official Hajj in Makkah. The events completed in today's Hajj remember the events of the past.

What happens on Hajj?

Preparations for Hajj

Preparing for Hajj is very important for Muslims. They must ensure they can afford it and are physically fit enough to complete the journey. They also need to make sure they have provided for their family at home. Muslims also may attend special lessons prior to going to Makkah in order to fully understand the challenge of completing the fifth Pillar.

Muslims first state their **niyyah** or intention of attending Hajj. They enter the state of **ihram** or holiness to ensure they present themselves in the correct state to complete the Hajj. Ihram also refers to the clothes that all Muslim pilgrims will wear on Hajj. This includes two pieces of white unsewn cloth for men; one is tied around the waist and the other is thrown over the shoulder. Women must be fully covered in a long-sleeved, ankle-length garment and have their heads covered. Muslims are not allowed to take personal belongings, or wear jewellery or perfume on the Hajj.

Actions performed on Hajj

Figure 2.13 Tawaf – walking around the Ka'bah during Hajj

1   Muslim pilgrims circle the Ka'bah in an anti-clockwise direction seven times. This action is known as **Tawaf**. It shows unity with Allah as all Muslims move in harmony with each other. In one corner of the Ka'bah is the **Black Stone**, which many Muslims will try to kiss or touch.

2   Muslims will move through a passage between the hills of Marwa and Safa seven times. This is called the **sa'y** and is done in remembrance of Hagar's search for water in the desert.

3   Pilgrims travel to **Mount Arafat** where they stand and beg forgiveness for their sins for a number of hours in the day. Many Muslims read from the Qur'an and perform their daily prayers there.

Figure 2.14 Pilgrims at Mount Arafat during Hajj

4   Pilgrims travel to **Mina** where they collect 49 pebbles. They throw these at three stone pillars to symbolise rejecting the devil.

5   Then, Muslim pilgrims sacrifice an animal, often a sheep or a goat, to remember the sacrifice Ibrahim was willing to make to Allah in sacrificing his son. Many Muslims may pay together for this and the meat is shared with as many people as possible, including the poor.

6   After the sacrifice, Muslim men shave their heads as a symbol of a new beginning, and women trim their hair.

As a final act, many Muslims return to Makkah and repeat the actions of Tawaf, circling the Ka'bah. Many Muslims choose to stay on in Saudi Arabia after completing Hajj to visit other historical sites of interest, such as the tomb of Muhammad.

Why is Hajj important?

• It is one of the Five Pillars and is therefore considered to be obligatory. This is highlighted in Surah 22:25–30.

Sources of authority

"And proclaim the Pilgrimage among men: they will come to you on foot and (mounted) on every kind of camel, lean on account of journeys through deep and distant mountain highways; That they may witness the benefits (provided) for them, and celebrate the name of Allah, through the Days appointed over the cattle which He has provided for them (for sacrifice): then eat ye thereof and feed the distressed ones in want. Then let them complete the rites prescribed for them, perform their vows and (again) circumambulate the Ancient House" (Surah 22:27–29)

- It shows equality between all Muslims. Everyone wears ihram, completes the same actions and stands before Allah as equals in their aim of completing Hajj.
- It is a ritual designed to unite Muslims as a community, known as ummah.
- It helps Muslims to renew their sense of purpose in the world. Hajj is a strenuous journey that they undertake for Allah.
- Makkah is the holy city for Muslims where much of the history of the religion began and so it is an important spiritual place for them to visit.

What are the benefits and challenges of Hajj?

Hajj helps Muslims to feel closer to Allah because they are performing one of the obligatory Pillars. It also allows them to trace the roots of their religion and reaffirm their belief in Allah and Islam. It strengthens them in their lives.

However, Hajj can be expensive. Some Muslims may never complete Hajj. Those who can afford to go more than once will sometimes contribute towards sending another Muslim. Hajj is also physically demanding and can be dangerous.

Activities ?

1 Think about a journey you made to a place you have always wanted to go. Why was this place important to you? Share your thoughts with a partner. Does your journey have any similarities to a pilgrimage? Explain why or why not.

2 Work in groups to write a list of questions you might ask a Muslim who has just returned from Hajj. Take it in turns to take the 'hot seat' and answer questions, offering the answers you think the person returning from Hajj might give.

Can you remember?

- What are the Five Pillars?
- Why was Makkah so important to Muhammad and what place did it have in his life?
- What is the importance of Makkah to the other Pillars of Islam?

Exam-style question

Explain two reasons why Hajj is so important for Muslims today. In your answer you must refer to a source of authority and wisdom. **(5 marks)**

Exam tip

This answer requires you to give two different reasons and you need to explain each one fully, perhaps giving examples or detailed explanation to illustrate the point you are making. You also are required to mention a source of authority or wisdom such as the Qur'an.

Summary

- Hajj is the fifth Pillar of Islam, which happens during the month of Dhul-Hijjah.
- It is considered a duty for Muslims to perform Hajj at least once in their lifetime.
- Muslims will enter a state of ihram for the entirety of Hajj.
- Muslims complete symbolic actions on Hajj including Tawaf, sa'y, standing on Mount Arafat, stoning the devil and animal sacrifice.
- Hajj is a strenuous journey and some Muslims die trying to complete it.

Checkpoint

Strengthen

S1 What is Hajj and how often should a Muslim complete it?

S2 Why do Muslims believe it is important for them to complete Hajj?

S3 What are the benefits and challenges of a Muslim completing Hajj?

Challenge

C1 How do you think a Muslim would feel after they have completed Hajj?

C2 What do you think a Muslim can learn about themselves from completing Hajj?

C3 Why might some people today not see any point in completing Hajj?

2.7 Jihad

Learning objectives

- To understand the origin, meaning and significance of jihad.
- To identify the similarities and differences between lesser and greater jihad.
- To understand the conditions needed for lesser jihad.
- To understand the importance of jihad in the life of Muslims.

Origin and meaning of 'jihad'

The Islamic term **jihad** literally translates to 'struggle' or 'striving.' This means to struggle or strive for Allah. Often, in today's world, the word jihad is associated with examples of war, conflict or terrorism. Traditionally, this term actually has three different meanings, as follows:

- a Muslim's individual struggle to follow the teachings of Islam and resist evil, often known as **greater jihad**
- the struggle to build a good community
- holy war or the struggle to defend Islam, often known as **lesser jihad**.

In the modern world there are many versions of what jihad means, including sacrificing yourself to Allah's will or struggling to achieve a noble cause. Many Muslims believe it is working to promote peace and co-operation. Muslims may place different emphasis on understanding jihad and be divergent in their application of the idea. Most Muslims recognise that jihad is a personal struggle rather than any form of war, recognising that in today's world, there are many temptations which must be resisted.

Greater jihad

Greater jihad is considered to be the most important form of jihad and refers to the effort of every Muslim to live their life as a Muslim as well as possible. This means living their life according to the rules of Allah and the Qur'an, doing everything they can to help those around them and resisting the things in life that may tempt them at times.

Muslims believe that they can get closer to Allah by performing greater jihad and trying to resist evil in the world around them. The Five Pillars of Islam are duties that they are expected to perform in order to achieve this.

Figure 2.15 A Muslim praying

Other actions they may do in their search to apply the principles of greater jihad in their lives include:

- learning the Qur'an off by heart
- taking part in Muslim community activities to try to strengthen the ummah
- working for **social justice**, where fairness is seen between all people and equality within the world
- forgiving those who have done wrong to them.

Lesser jihad

Islam is a peaceful religion but even those who support ideas of peace can find themselves in situations of conflict. Muslims believe that all peaceful methods should be tried to resolve conflict before resorting to any kind of fighting, but lesser jihad is often interpreted as holy war.

Muslims believe that Muhammad taught his followers that Muslims should defend Islam and there are many stories that he himself led others into battle. However, Muslims believe that although there may be occasions when violence should be used as a last resort in order to achieve peace, there are strict requirements before embarking on any sort of holy war. These are listed below.

1 War must be declared by a religious leader.
2 The opponent should always have started the fighting so Muslims fight in self-defence.
3 Reasons for jihad include: self-defence, to strengthen Islam, protecting the rights of Muslims to practice their religion and protecting Muslims against oppression.
4 It must be fought to bring about good and not evil.
5 It should be a last resort.
6 Innocent people should not be killed.
7 Enemies should be treated with justice and mercy, as Islam is a peaceful and compassionate religion.

Significance of jihad

Jihad is important to Muslims because:

- they accept that greater jihad, as the daily struggle against temptation faced by Muslims, was considered to be more important by Muhammad
- they believe every Muslim faces a daily battle to resist evil in the world
- jihad is seen as an act of sacrifice. It may mean Muslims have to sacrifice their time, skills, money or even their life for Allah
- they believe there are some occasions when fighting is the right action.

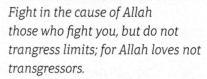

Sources of authority

Fight in the cause of Allah those who fight you, but do not trangress limits; for Allah loves not transgressors.

And slay them wherever you catch them, and turn them out from where they have turned you out; for tumult and oppression are worse than slaughter; but fight them not at the Sacred Mosque, unless they (first) fight you there; but if they fight you, slay them. Such is the reward of those who suppress faith.

But if they cease, Allah is Oft-Forgiving, Most Merciful.

And fight them on until there is no more tumult or oppression, and there prevail justice and faith in Allah; but if they cease, let there be no hostility except to those who practise oppression. (Surah 2:190–194)

To those against whom war is made, permission is given (to fight), because they are wronged;–and verily, Allah is Most Powerful for their aid. (Surah 22:39)

Activities

1 Make a list of the things you struggle with in your daily life. Explain how you try to resist them.
2 Consider what you know about Islam and how Muslims live their life. Create a presentation on the daily struggles a Muslim might encounter in their life.
3 'Life is a test.' Consider this statement. With a partner, discuss any arguments you can think of to agree and disagree with it. Join with another pair and debate which arguments are stronger and why. Try to include the idea of jihad in some of your arguments.
4 Muslims sometimes view jihad as 'the sixth Pillar of Islam'. Do you think jihad is so important that it should be put alongside the other Five Pillars? Discuss this issue with a group. At the end, present your overall conclusion to the class after considering all of your group's arguments.

Exam-style question

In this question, 3 of the marks awarded will be for your spelling, punctuation and grammar and your use of specialist terminology.

'War is never justified.' Evaluate this statement, considering arguments for and against. In your response you should refer to Muslim teachings to reach a justified conclusion.

(12 marks)

Exam tip

This question covers war and you need to be sensitive about the arguments you include. Remember that as part of your answer you have to show awareness of Islamic teachings and beliefs. To do this, you will need to show the complexity of the idea of jihad and how it is seen to have different meanings.

Summary

- Jihad means 'striving' for Allah.
- Muslims understand that there are three main types of jihad.
- Greater jihad is a personal struggle in which each Muslim has to live their life as Allah wants and resist evil.
- Greater jihad also covers the idea of a struggle to try to build a strong Islamic ummah, community.
- Lesser jihad is understood as holy war but it has various conditions attached to it in order for holy war to be justified.

Checkpoint

Strengthen

S1 What does jihad mean and what types of jihad are there?

S2 What does each Source of authority quote say about jihad?

S3 Why is greater jihad more important to Muslims than lesser jihad?

Challenge

C1 Why do you think many people, including Muslims, might say that war is never justified?

C2 How easy or difficult do you think a Muslim finds greater jihad and why?

C3 Why might greater jihad be something every person struggles with today and not just Muslims?

2.8 Celebrations and commemorations

Learning objectives

- To understand the nature, origins and activities of Id-ul-Adha and Id-ul-Fitr in Sunni Islam.
- To understand the nature, origins and activities of Id-ul-Ghadeer and Ashura in Shi'a Islam.
- To explore the significance of these celebrations.

Muslims believe that it is important to remember, celebrate and commemorate events that have happened in the history of the religion. The Islamic word 'Id' means 'celebration'. All Muslims recognise and celebrate the two main Islamic festivals of **Id-ul-Adha** and Id-ul-Fitr. Shi'a Muslims also commemorate **Id-ul-Ghadeer** and **Ashura**.

Figure 2.16 Celebration cards for Id-ul-Fitr and Id-ul-Adha

Id-ul-Adha

Id-ul-Adha means 'Festival of Sacrifice'. It is a festival that remembers the Prophet Ibrahim's demonstration of faith and trust in Allah. Ibrahim's faith was tested when Allah commanded that he sacrifice his son. Ibrahim trusted God completely and prepared to carry out his will. Before Ibrahim sacrificed Isaac, Allah provided a ram to be killed

Figure 2.17 Celebrating Id-ul-Adha

in his place (Surah 37: 77–111). This story is also found within the Abrahamic religions of Judaism and Christianity.

Muslims celebrate this story because it also reminds them of the importance of developing faith and trust in Allah. This festival also happens at the end of Hajj, the fifth Pillar of Islam, which further reinforces its significance within the Islamic year. It links Muslims completing Hajj with their spiritual city and the ummah of Muslims all over the world will celebrate together. Those celebrating the festival of Id-ul-Adha will think of those completing Hajj and also share in their achievement.

Today, in Muslim countries, Id-ul-Adha is a public holiday. Muslims usually organise for the sacrifice of an animal as a reminder of Ibrahim's agreement to sacrifice his son. The meat is shared among friends and family and some is given to those in need so they too can share in the festival celebration. Special prayers will be spoken at the mosque and cards and presents will be given. Often extra money is donated to the poor.

Id-ul-Fitr

Id-ul-Fitr means 'Festival of breaking the fast' and is a celebration that takes place at the end of Ramadan. It signifies the end of Muslims performing the fourth Pillar of Islam, which is Sawm. This is when Muslims fast during the daylight hours of the month of Ramadan.

The first Id is believed to have been celebrated by Muhammad in 624 CE with his friends. Muslims believe that they are celebrating the end of fasting. They are also thanking Allah for the strength he gave them to complete this Pillar since it takes determination and self-discipline in order to achieve this.

Muslims will buy new clothes to wear and attend special services in the mosque. This brings the Islamic ummah together. There may be processions through the streets and a celebratory atmosphere. Muslims will of course join with friends and family to share a special meal that has been prepared. Cards and presents may also be given.

Id-ul-Ghadeer

Shi'a Muslims recognise and celebrate the festival of Id-ul-Ghadeer on 18 Zilhajj. It remembers the appointment of **Ali ibn Abi Talib** by Muhammad as his successor. As there is some disagreement between Sunni and Shi'a Muslims over the authority of succession in Islam after the death of Muhammad, this festival is not recognised by Sunni Muslims. In Shi'a Islam, Muhammad is believed to have announced Ali as his successor, as told by Allah. Shi'as also believe that immediately after the announcement it was revealed that Allah had perfected the religion of Islam. They understand this as confirming that Ali is the rightful successor according to Allah.

Shi'a Muslims believe that this is a significant event for them to mark because it shows them the line of leadership within the religion. It also reinforces the

Sources of authority

…This day I have perfected for you your religion and completed My favour upon you and have approved for you Islam as your religion… (Surah 5:3)

importance of Muhammad acting to continue to guide them through his choice of successor. They often celebrate this festival by fasting or by sharing food with the poor. They will spend time thanking Allah and Muhammad for ensuring the succession of Islam.

Ashura

Ashura is a celebration recognised by both Shi'a and Sunni Muslims. It takes place on the tenth day of **Muharram**, the first month of the Islamic calendar. For Shi'a Muslims, Ashura is a solemn commemoration of the martyrdom at Karbala in 680 CE of Hussain, who was a grandson of the Prophet Muhammad. He was killed in battle with his followers.

There are often mourning rituals and passion plays that retell the stories. Shi'a Muslims may dress in black and parade through the streets. For Sunni Muslims, Ashura is a fasting day which remembers how **Nuh** left the Ark and how **Musa** was saved from the Egyptians by Allah. It appears to have less historical significance as a festival in Sunni Islam whereas Shi'a Muslims consider this festival celebration to be commemorating their history.

Figure 2.18 Celebrating Ashura

Why are these celebrations important to Muslims?

- They mark and remember significant events in the history of Islam.
- They are a way for Muslims to connect to the past and ensure their history is not forgotten.
- These events still have significance today in helping Muslims to understand their religion and live their lives as Allah intends them to.
- Muslims believe celebrating special occasions will bring them closer to Allah.
- Celebrations and festivals help to reinforce the ummah. All Muslims share in the festivals and their shared beliefs of their religion.

Activities ?

1 Make a list of five things you celebrate in your life. How do you celebrate these events and why? Share your thoughts with a partner and discuss why and how it is important to celebrate events.

2 Write a conversation between a Muslim and a non-Muslim explaining the main celebrations in Islam and the reasons behind celebrating them.

3 Divide the class in half and debate the following statement as a class: 'There is no point in celebrating festivals today.' Each group should spend some time planning the arguments to include in the debate. Once you have presented all the arguments, vote as a class on the side you feel offered the best arguments.

Can you remember?

- How do the pillars of Sawm and Hajj relate to the festivals of Id-ul-Adha and Id-ul-Fitr?
- Why is it important to Muslims to recognise the history of Islam?
- Why do Muslims believe the prophets are so important in Islam?

Exam-style question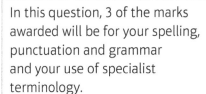

In this question, 3 of the marks awarded will be for your spelling, punctuation and grammar and your use of specialist terminology.

'Celebrations help to bring people together.' Evaluate this statement, considering arguments for and against. in your response you should

- refer to Muslim teachings
- reach a justified conclusion.

(15 marks)

Exam tip

You need to consider the statement in the question carefully before you attempt to write your answer. Think carefully about your own opinion, as well as what other views may be. The question requires you to refer to Islam in your answer, so re-read this topic and consider what a Muslim might say and why.

Summary

- Celebrations and commemorations are important in Islam.
- All Muslims celebrate the two main festivals of Id-ul-Adha and Id-ul-Fitr.
- Shi'a Muslims also celebrate Id-ul-Ghadeer and Ashura.
- Celebrations help to unite Muslims and their beliefs.

Checkpoint

Strengthen

S1 What does 'Id' mean?
S2 What do the festivals of Id-ul-Adha and Id-ul-Fitr celebrate?
S3 What do the Shi'a festivals of Id-ul-Ghadeer and Ashura celebrate?

Challenge

C1 Why do you think different branches of Islam recognise different festival celebrations?
C2 What can we learn about Muslims from the way they celebrate their festivals?
C3 Why might some people today say that celebrating festivals has no place in modern society?

Recap: Living the Muslim life

Use the activities and exam-style questions on the following pages to reinforce your learning before you move on to the next chapter.

Recap quiz

Ten Obligatory Acts of Shi'a Islam

1 What are the Ten Obligatory Acts for Shi'a Muslims?
2 Why are the Ten Obligatory Acts important for Shi'a Muslims?
3 Name the Five Pillars of Islam in the correct order.
4 Why are the Five Pillars of Islam important?
5 How will performing the Five Pillars of Islam impact upon the life of a Muslim?

Shahadah as one of the Five Pillars

6 What two beliefs are contained in the Shahadah?
7 Why is the Shahadah so important to Muslims?

Salah as one of the Five Pillars

8 How many times a day should Muslims pray?
9 What must Muslims do before they pray to ensure they are prepared?
10 What is the purpose of Salah for Muslims today?
11 What is the Friday prayer service in the mosque called?

Sawm as one of the Five Pillars

12 What is the name of the month when Muslims perform Sawm?
13 Why do Muslims perform Sawm?
14 Who does not have to take part in Sawm?
15 Why is the Night of Power significant to Muslims today?

Zakah as one of the Five Pillars and Khums

16 What is Khums?
17 How much money is given annually in Zakah?
18 Why do Muslims feel it is important to give Zakah?
19 Why is Khums important for Shi'a Muslims?

Hajj as one of the Five Pillars

20 Where do Muslims go to perform Hajj?
21 What are the main actions Muslims perform while on Hajj?
22 What is the state of holiness Muslims enter on Hajj called?
23 What is the significance of Hajj for Muslims today?
24 Why can completing Hajj be seen as a challenge for some Muslims today?

Jihad

25 What does 'jihad' literally mean?
26 What are greater and lesser jihad?
27 What conditions are there for lesser jihad?
28 What are the key differences between greater and lesser jihad?
29 Why do Muslims feel greater jihad is more important than lesser jihad?

Celebrations and commemorations

30 What does the festival of Id-ul-Adha celebrate?
31 When does Id-ul-Fitr take place and why?
32 Which branch of Islam celebrates the festivals of Id-ul-Ghadeer and Ashura?
33 Why do Muslims celebrate Id-ul-Fitr and Id-ul-Adha today?

Activities ?

1 Create a summary diagram of each topic in this chapter covering the 5Ws: Who? What? When? Where? Why?

2 Make a list of any new terms you have come across in this chapter. Create flashcards to add to those you created in the previous chapter. Use these with a partner to test each other's knowledge of what they mean.

3 Which of the topics in this chapter do you think a Muslim would say is most important and why? Think of a list of reasons for your view, making sure you explain and develop each idea fully. Present these to a partner to see if they agree with you or not.

4 Debate the following statement: 'There are so many rules and things you have to follow in Islam that it would be difficult to follow them all.' Come up with arguments for and against.

5 Write a conversation between a non-Muslim and a Muslim about what it is like to live a Muslim life. Try to focus on including all the new information you have covered in this chapter, as well as referring to any information previously studied about Islam. Act it out with a partner. Record it and use it in your revision.

Exam-style questions

- Outline three features of Hajj. **(3 marks)**
- Explain two reasons why greater jihad is important to Muslims. **(4 marks)**
- Explain two reasons why the Five Pillars of Islam are so important to Muslims. In your answer you should refer to a source of wisdom and authority. **(5 marks)**
- In this question, 3 of the marks awarded will be for your spelling, punctuation and grammar and your use of specialist terminology.

  Evaluate this statement considering arguments for and against. In your response you should
  o refer to Muslim teachings
  o reach a justified conclusion. **(15 marks)**

Exam tips

- Each question has a 'command' word, which instructs you in what you have to do. Examples include: outline; explain; assess; evaluate. Make sure you look at the command word carefully to make sure you understand what the question is asking.
- Read each question carefully before starting to answer it. If appropriate, take some time to plan out your answer to decide what knowledge it is important to include.
- Make sure you practise each style of question carefully to familiarise yourself with how you should answer it.
- Consider carefully the wording of every question and task you are asked to complete. Create a success criteria checklist, which you can refer back to at the end of the questions to check you have covered all the requirements.
- Key words are crucial when you are completing written answers. You need to ensure you know what the key word means, spell it correctly, use it appropriately and define it clearly if required.

Extend: Living the Muslim life

Source

Diary of Hajj by Ahmed

DAY 1 – arriving in Makkah

We've arrived in Saudi Arabia and are waiting in Jeddah airport for our transport to arrive and take us to the holy city of Makkah. After getting through border control and getting our free Hajj gifts, zamzam water and some provisions for while we are here, we get on the coach and finally we are on our way.

We arrive at the hotel and we are very close to the Grand Mosque, Masjid al Haram, which is built around the Ka'bah. Although Hajj doesn't start for a couple of days I am eager to go to see the Ka'bah. I feel a sense of excitement at being in Makkah but am also nervous. I am a little unsure about the challenge that faces me and if I am strong enough to complete it.

DAYS 2 and 3 – Makkah

I spend the next couple of days in Makkah, taking in the atmosphere. Seeing the Ka'bah is surreal and I get a shiver every time I look at it. As time passes, more and more people start to arrive – from all over the world and all nationalities. It makes me realise how worldwide a religion Islam is. I spend a lot of time in the Mosque praying to Allah and reflecting on why I am here, in such a holy place.

DAYS 4–8 – Dhul Hijjah (the start of Hajj)

Hajj officially begins with all Muslims adopting the state of ihram. It is an amazing feeling to see everyone dressed the same way and know they are here for the same reason. I feel really humble and it is a great sight to see so many people. I perform Tawaf, which means circling the Ka'bah seven times. This is really difficult as there are so many people. I want to be closer to it but that just isn't possible. Next it's the sa'y, which is running between the hills of Mawa and Safa to remember the desperation Hagar felt at trying to find water. Every action completed on Hajj is an opportunity to remember important events within the religion and to reflect on their significance. I then travel to Mina, which is where I will stay until tomorrow. I chat to some of the people from my group and already I feel we have a connection. Some of the day is spent in prayer, reflecting on why I am here and how I am submitting to Allah.

DAYS 5–9 – Mount Arafat

Today, I will spend the day on Mount Arafat, praising Allah and thanking him. Today I feel close to Allah. I know that this is where Islam believes mankind will gather on the Day of Judgement, where Allah will decide each person's fate. This is a sobering thought and makes me consider my actions in life and how I feel about the things I have done wrong. Towards the end of the day, my group go to Muzdalifah, where we collect stones. These are for the ritual of stoning the pillars.

DAYS 6–10 – Jamarat Bridge

After only a few hours' sleep and rest, I am ready to go again and perform the next ritual. We are at the Jamarat Bridge in Mina and I have my stones ready to throw at the pillars. This symbolises rejecting the devil and remembers the story of Ibrahim rejecting the devil. I thought this would be a difficult challenge and was a little scared as, on previous occasions, people have even been killed completing this task. However, it wasn't as bad as I thought and the ritual action really made me think carefully about how I can reject temptation within my life. On this day, an important Islamic festival – Id-ul-Adha – is also being celebrated by Muslims all over the world. This makes me think of my family at home and I am certain they will be thinking about me. All the pilgrims joined together to sacrifice an animal here, just as our families at home would be doing. Some of the meat is shared with the poor, which shows how we should all care for each other. After this has happened, I have to shave my head. This symbolises that I am sincere in my submission to Allah. I'm not sure my new look suits me!

DAYS 7–11 – Jamarat Bridge

Today isn't as busy as the last few days. I spend some time in prayer before it is time to complete the ritual of stoning the devil again. If anything, this seems more important today. The atmosphere is electric with so many people there all shouting their defiance of the devil.

DAYS 8–12 – Makkah

I am now back in Makkah and my time here is coming to an end. I complete Tawaf again. Makkah is much busier now than it was a few days ago and there seem to be people everywhere – young and old. It is an amazing experience and it makes me proud to be Muslim.

DAY 9 – Returning home

It has been a fantastic experience and one that I will never forget! I've met some fascinating people and really learned a lot, both about myself and my religion. It was incredible to see so many people in the same place, at the same time, performing the same actions. There were no barriers between us; we were all equal in our quest to complete the fifth Pillar of Islam, seek forgiveness from Allah and get closer to him. It really was a once in a lifetime opportunity and for me, the greatest trip on Earth!

Activities ?

1. Make a list of all the Islamic terms used by Ahmed in his account of Hajj. Explain each term.

2. Make a list of the rituals Ahmed performs while completing Hajj. What does each one symbolise or remember?

3. Write down the emotions you think Ahmed experiences on this journey and what may be making him feel each one. Why do you think this is such an emotional journey for a Muslim?

4. How are the ideas of peace, equality and Tawhid shown through Hajj?

5. How important do you think it is for a Muslim to complete Hajj? What evidence is there in Ahmed's account of his Hajj experience to support your view?

6. Remind yourself of each of the Five Pillars of Islam. Consider how easy or difficult each Pillar is to complete, including the Pillar of Hajj. Why do you think Muslims go to so much effort to complete the Pillars?

7. How does performing the Five Pillars of Islam, especially Hajj, demonstrate ideas of greater jihad? Make sure you give examples to explain your answer.

8. In groups, create and perform a radio chat show interview with Ahmed to ask him questions about his experience of Hajj. Make sure you use his thoughts in his diary to consider how he might answer each question.

9. Choose one of the following statements and in a group, plan and hold a debate:
   a 'Hajj today is out of date and not relevant.'
   b 'It is more important for a Muslim to pray five times a day than to try to complete the journey of Hajj.'
   c 'Festivals today should not include animal sacrifice.'

Figure 2.19 The Mosque in Makkah during the Hajj

Exam tips

- When answering questions, make sure you first take the time to work out what the question is asking you to do. Remember that you are required to demonstrate knowledge and understanding, so you need to ensure you consider the question carefully.

- When you are asked to consider creating arguments for a debate or to offer your own opinion, make sure you think carefully about what counter-arguments may be offered. This will help you to improve the quality of your own responses.

- Punctuation is important, so don't forget to use it. This includes capital letters, full stops and commas, as well as question marks.

Can you remember?

- What are the names of the Five Pillars of Islam? Why are the Five Pillars of Islam important to Muslims?

- What do Muslims believe about Allah and how does this belief affect their daily lives?

- Why is Muhammad so important to Islam?

- What is the significance of the holy city of Makkah?

- Why do Muslims believe it is important to trace the roots and history of their religion?

- Why are beliefs and practices important to Muslims?

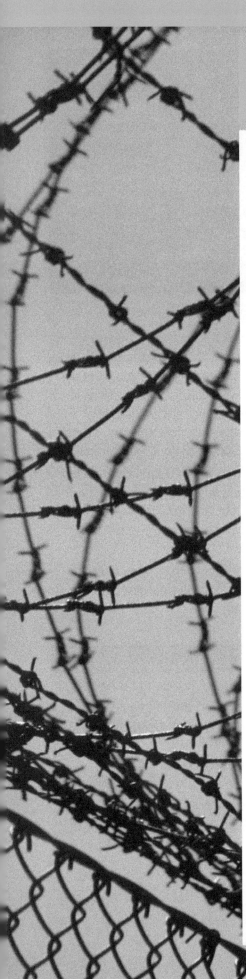

3 Crime and punishment

In today's world, crime and punishment are prominent and growing issues. The nature of crime may be evolving with the changing nature of society, but this is leading to a range of other problems. The media regularly reports on issues associated with justice, crime, punishment and forgiveness, highlighting them as concerns for everyone. Islam, too, believes that these ideas are important and advocates that Muslims should stand up in society against injustices such as crime, to try to bring peace to the world.

Islam teaches that justice is important. Muslims accept that all humans deserve to be treated equally and fairly since Allah created them this way. They also believe that the Qur'an teaches that justice is an important idea to work towards. Muslims recognise that crime is a problem in society today and they try to work to lessen the impact of the causes of crime.

Muslims live their lives in the belief that this life is a test for the afterlife. They will always try to consider what they believe is the right action to take, according to their religion, in all situations they face. They believe that after death Allah will judge them based on their actions in this life. This idea has an impact on Muslim beliefs and actions. Some Muslims work to improve society by lessening the impact of crime and ensuring that people get justice wherever possible. Muslims do not necessarily believe it is their place to judge others, as they are taught by Islam that Allah is the judge who will decide whether a person is suitable to go to al-Jannah in the afterlife. Many Muslims believe that the laws of a country are important and if these are broken, a person should expect the necessary punishment. Many Muslims also recognise Shari'ah law which they view as the laws of Allah. This too, can be used by Muslim in cases where it appears laws have been broken. Many Muslim countries will use this in determining the appropriate punishments.

Muslims accept that punishment has an important role in society when a crime has been committed. They recognise that punishment can help to bring about change and reform offenders. It also helps to keep people safe and make society feel protected. Muslims believe that when a person has committed a crime, it is important for them to face a suitable punishment that is relative to the crime they committed. They accept that ideas of justice apply to both the victim and the offender.

Forgiveness is an important idea practised within Islam. Muslims believe that Allah is merciful and forgiving and they should therefore follow his example. Although they understand that some actions are difficult to forgive, they believe forgiveness is important in trying to strengthen society and unite people across the world. It allows those who have been wronged to move on, and those who have done wrong to be forgiven and accepted back into society.

Although Muslims accept ideas of justice and forgiveness, they are divided on their views about the use of **capital punishment** as a form of justice. It can be especially difficult for Muslims who live in the UK to follow the laws of the country when their religion may teach something that seems to go against this. Issues such as capital punishment have no universal rules and it is often up to the individual to decide what action they believe is right. Islam provides guidance on issues such as this so that Muslims can lead their lives as they believe Allah wishes. The religion of Islam has an impact on the daily life of every Muslim. It influences their beliefs, and the way they may act and behave in issues concerning crime and punishment.

Learning objectives

In this chapter you will find out about Muslim:

- attitudes towards crime and justice
- actions to end the causes of crime
- teachings about good, evil and suffering
- attitudes towards punishment
- attitudes towards the aims of punishment
- teachings about forgiveness
- teachings about the treatment of criminals
- attitudes towards the death penalty.

Checkpoint

Recall

Before starting this chapter, you should remember:

- Allah is important to Muslims and they consider him in everything they do
- Muslim beliefs about Allah and the religion of Islam will influence the way they may behave and act in society
- Muslims refer to sources of authority, such as the Qur'an and Muhammad, in order to help them make decisions concerning issues about crime and punishment
- Muslims hold very strong beliefs about the afterlife and how their actions and behaviour on Earth will impact on this
- Muslims may not all hold the same views on issues such as crime and punishment
- Muslims may interpret the teachings of Islam differently and follow them to varying degrees
- Muslims live in different countries across the world, where the law on issues such as crime and punishment may differ.

Look ahead

In future chapters you will find out about:

- Islamic beliefs and attitudes towards peace and conflict
- Islamic beliefs about living a religious life.

3.1 Crime and justice

Learning objectives

- To understand the nature of justice and its importance to Muslims.
- To consider why justice is important for the victim.

Justice is the idea that each person has the right to fair treatment in whatever circumstance. It is a term that can be applied in many contexts and situations, although it is commonly linked with crime and punishment. Often people feel that justice is achieved when a person who has committed a crime is punished suitably and 'gets what they deserve'.

Justice is an important idea in a functioning society. Rules and laws are created in order to maintain order and ensure that everyone is treated equally and fairly. Laws serve to protect and try to ensure justice. In terms of crime and punishment, laws are there to set out what is and is not acceptable. When laws are broken it is expected that there will be a suitable punishment for criminals at the end of the legal process.

Islam teaches its followers not only to be just, but to be just even in the face of strong conflicting emotions. There may be times when justice is difficult but Muslims are taught that it is always the right thing.

Justice is seen in many actions performed by Muslims. They believe that they should share what they have with others. This is known as the Pillar of Zakah, when Muslims are expected to give 2.5 per cent of their residual wealth to help the poor and needy. Justice is a common idea seen within the celebration of Islamic festivals. Muslims sacrifice animals at Id-ul-Adha and Id-ul-Fitr and share the meat with the poor, showing the fair treatment of all people.

Why is justice important to Muslims?

Justice is an idea that is seen to capture the essence of all Islamic teachings and runs through all Islamic values and actions. It is seen in the Five Pillars of Islam and the way in which Allah commands Muslims to live their lives. It is important because:

- Muslims believe that Allah is the sole creator of the universe and he created all humans to be equal, whatever their race, culture or gender. Therefore, all people deserve equality and justice in the way they are treated
- Muslims believe that Allah is just. They believe that he will treat everyone with justice and fairness and Muslims believe they too should act this way. Many names of Allah relate to ideas of justice, including The Judge and The Giver of Justice
- The Qur'an teaches the importance of justice and how Allah intended for justice within society.

Figure 3.1 The scales of justice

As Surah 4:135 below shows, Muslims believe they have been commanded by Allah to stand up for justice in society. Islam is a religion of submission to Allah and this includes standing up against the wrongs in society in order to bring peace.

Sources of authority

O you who believe! stand out firmly for justice, as witnesses to Allah, even as against yourselves, or your parents, or your kin, and whether it be (against) rich or poor: for Allah can best protect both. Follow not the lusts (of your hearts), lest you swerve, and if you distort (justice) or decline to do justice, verily Allah is well acquainted with all that you do. (Surah 4:135)

Muslims believe that on the Day of Judgement after death, all humans will be judged by Allah. It is accepted by Muslims that those who are good and just will enter al-Jannah, Paradise, and those who are unjust will go to Jahannam, Hell.

Muslims follow the teachings of **Shari'ah law**, which is the Islamic code of behaviour. This teaches that all Muslims are equal under the law and deserve fairness in the way they are treated.

The importance of justice for the victim

Justice and fairness are ideas accepted by both non-religious people and religious believers and is the Islamic idea of paradise in the afterlife. It seems right for people to be treated in the same way. It also seems right for a person who has done something wrong to be punished for this wrong action, something we are all taught as children by our parents.

When a crime is committed, many people may be affected both directly and indirectly. The victim is the person who is most directly affected. They are at the centre of what has happened and may have been hurt or even killed in the crime. It is vitally important for victims to feel that their pain and suffering have been recognised, and to know that the person who caused it has been punished. Therefore, it is very important that victims feel they have received justice for what happened to them.

Non-religious attitudes

Justice is not simply a religious idea – it is an idea that is promoted within society by people who are both religious and non-religious. Atheists may feel that justice is important as it equates to fair treatment for all and demonstrates ideas of equality and the importance of each and every human.

For Humanists, recognition of equality, justice and equal dignity and treatment of humans underpins many of their ideas and standpoints. Humanists aims to try and strive for a world of mutual care and concern which gives peace, justice and opportunity to everyone. Although their ideas are not based on religious beliefs, they feel justice is important within society.

In response to this, many Muslims would recognise that although they share beliefs about the importance of the concept of justice, Muslims believe it is important because Allah is fair and wants justice for the world.

Sources of authority

Allah commands justice, the doing of good, and liberality to kith and kin… (Surah 16:90)

O you who believe! Stand out firmly for Allah as witnesses to fair dealing, and let not the hatred of others to you make you swerve to wrong and depart from justice… (Surah 5:8)

We sent aforetime our messengers with Clear Signs and sent down with them the Book and the Balance (of Right and Wrong), that men may stand forth in justice… (Surah 57:25)

Figure 3.2 Victims need to feel they have received justice

Can you remember?

- Which of the names of Allah relate to ideas of justice?
- How are ideas of justice shown within the Five Pillars of Islam?

Activities ?

1. Write a story of no more than 200 words called 'Justice!' about a crime and the punishment given for it. In your story, make sure you show your understanding of the term 'justice', as well as showing Islamic understandings of justice and why Muslims feel it is important.

2. Look at each of the quotes from the Qur'an on justice. In your own words, summarise what you think each one is saying and explain how it relates to Muslim ideas about justice.

3. Do you think justice is the most important idea for Muslims? Use your previous knowledge to help you answer this question. Share your ideas with a partner, discussing and debating its importance for Muslims, considering how it may relate to other important ideas within Islam.

Exam-style question

Outline three reasons why justice is important for Muslims. **(3 marks)**

Extend your knowledge

Shari'ah law means 'way' or 'path' and is the legal framework or code of behaviour for Islam. It deals with many topics, including crime, politics, marriage contracts and economics, as well as personal issues such as diet, prayer and fasting. Shari'ah law is derived from the Qur'an and Hadith, the words and actions of the Prophet Muhammad. There has been some controversy in how Shari'ah law is applied, especially when its guidance on issues such as crime and punishment seem to conflict with secular law or the laws of the country where Muslims live. Shari'ah law is not recognised in the UK and the laws of the country, set by the Government, take precedence.

Exam tip

You are asked to give three different reasons to answer this question successfully. Try to write three separate sentences giving a different reason in each one.

Summary

- Justice is when fair treatment is applied.
- Allah is seen to treat people justly and Muslims believe they should do the same.
- Muslims believe they will be judged after death on the Day of Judgement on their actions in life and they should try to live their lives in a just way.
- Justice is seen within Islamic beliefs and practices.
- Justice for the victim of a crime means that they feel their crime has been dealt with appropriately.
- Punishment can be seen as a form of justice.

Checkpoint

Strengthen

S1 What is justice?

S2 Why is justice important for Muslims?

S3 How can punishment be seen as justice?

Challenge

C1 Why might some people not see some punishments as justice for the crimes committed?

C2 Why do you think the victim is not the only person who needs consideration when it comes to justice?

C3 Why do you think sometimes justice can be a difficult idea to apply to some situations?

3.2 Action to end the causes of crime

Learning objectives

- To understand the nature and problem of crime and Muslim attitudes towards it.
- To explore the reasons why crime might occur.
- To consider the action taken by Muslim individuals and groups to end these causes.

The nature and problem of crime

Each country imposes laws in order to have an ordered society and to keep its citizens safe. A crime is an act that is an offence against society that can be punished according to the law. It is generally considered to be a big problem within society. The nature of crime can vary enormously from minor acts of theft, lying or offensive behaviour to crimes that impact more seriously on individuals, such as assault, drug offences or murder. Today, new types of crime such as cyber-crime cause added problems for law enforcement organisations as they develop new methods of tackling crime and achieving justice for victims. Youth crime is also a growing problem and needs to be dealt with differently according to the age of the offender.

Why does crime occur?

Figure 3.3 Imprisonment – punishment for crime

There are many reasons why crimes are committed and often there is a combination of reasons. These include social, environmental or psychological reasons. Some crimes are committed out of desperation, while others may be thought through and planned by the offender. Some causes of crime are listed on the right.

Poverty

Poverty is the state of being poor or being unable to provide for oneself. Unemployment can lead to poverty, which in turn may lead to homelessness, and a lack of basic necessities, which can result in some people turning to crime to try to survive. It can become a vicious circle where people want to stop committing crimes but can't because of their situation.

Politics

Some people who are part of a political organisation or group may take advantage of others through their power. This may lead some to turn to crime in order to cope with their situations. It may also be the case that when one political group holds power in a country this can lead to an increase in crime, as the policies they impose impact negatively on people's lives and they find no alternative but to turn to crime to survive.

Racism

Racism is discrimination or treating a person differently because of their nationality, accent or the colour of their skin and remains a serious issue in the world today. Racism has contributed to unrest in parts of the world and there are still many who feel that some people don't deserve equal treatment. Racism is a crime in the UK, and in England and Wales there were 42,930 race crimes recorded by the police in 2014–15, and it is thought that many more incidents went unreported.

Drugs

People who are addicted to drugs can turn to crime to find money to pay for their drugs. Drug dealing is a crime and dealers are criminals who may encourage others to turn to a life of drugs and crime.

Upbringing

A person's **upbringing** can be a reason for them turning to crime. Many things may happen in families or at home that can lead people to turn to crime. It may be that a person is searching for love and attention that they did not receive in the family unit or their family is already involved in aspects of crime and they follow their example.

Low self-esteem

Low self-esteem can lead a person to turn to crime. A person who has low self-esteem has a lack of understanding of their value and worth and so may turn to crime to make them feel better in the short term. After failures in their life in certain areas, such as work, school or their home life, they may be searching for something to help. This can often lead to antisocial or criminal behaviour in society, such as drinking too much alcohol, or acting aggressively towards others.

Sources of authority

Allah commands justice, the doing of good, and liberality to kith and kin, and He forbids all shameful deeds, and injustice and rebellion: He instructs you, that you may receive admonition. Fulfil the Covenant of Allah when you have entered into it, and break not your oaths after you have confirmed them; indeed you have made Allah your surety; for Allah knows all that you do. And be not like a woman who breaks into untwisted strands the yarn which she has spun, after it has become strong. Nor take your oaths to practise deception between yourselves, lest one party should be more numerous than another: for Allah will test you by this; and on the Day of Judgement He will certainly make clear to you (the truth of) that wherein you disagree. (Surah 16:90-92)

Muslim teachings on crime

Muslims believe it is important they individually work to end the causes of crime, as they believe the ummah is important and all Muslims have a duty from Allah to care for others. As part of this:

- they believe that being involved in crime distracts them from what is important in life – worshipping Allah. Muslims believe that their time is put to better use through living their life as Allah intended
- they want to follow the example of Muhammad, who taught about the importance of helping others
- they believe their actions will help determine their afterlife. When Allah judges them on the Day of Judgement, they believe their actions will be taken into account as to whether they lived their life as Allah wanted them to
- tackling the causes of crime may prevent others from getting into situations associated with crime
- they are taught that all humans were created by Allah as equals and all deserve equal treatment.

Muslim Chaplains' Association

Mosaic is a mentoring organisation founded by HRH The Prince of Wales in 2007 to create opportunities for young people growing up in the most deprived areas of the UK, with a particular focus on those from Muslim communities. Mosaic's aim is to try and work to help all young people realise their potential. Through its ex-offender programme, Mosaic attempts to help reduce the causes of crime and prevent its young people from turning to crime as a solution to the problems they face.

Mosaic works with its beneficiaries to:

- mentor them whilst in education to raise their aspirations and encourage them to fully engage in education to have the best possible chance
- help those in prison who are Muslim to mentor offenders before they are released back into society and provide support for a period of time once back in society to help them adjust
- help provide opportunities and opening for young people to realise their capabilities and make the most of their lives.

The MCA is trying to reduce the impact of factors that can lead to crime in the first place in Muslim communities. They are also trying to stop those who have already turned to crime from being dragged into a cycle of re offending.

Mosaic is an organisation that works in the most deprived communities. Its aim is to help all young people realise their potential and in doing so help tackle the causes of crime.

Figure 3.4 Mosaic is a charity that provides mentoring programmes for young people

Activities

1   'Crime is the biggest problem faced by the world today.' Write a list of arguments that agree and disagree with this statement.

2   Prepare a presentation for younger children about the dangers of crime. Make sure you explain what the causes of crime are and refer to Islam when talking about the work done to tackle these.

3   Look at the websites of the MCA and Mosaic to see what projects they have been involved in that link to tackling the causes of crime. Create a summary diagram that explains the work they do.

Summary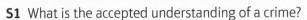

- A crime is an offence committed against the law of a country.
- The causes of crime include: poverty, politics, racism, drugs, upbringing and low self-esteem.
- Many Muslim individuals and groups, such as the MCA and Mosaic, work to try to tackle the causes of crime.

Can you remember?

- What do Muslims teach about justice?
- Why do Muslims believe that it is important to try to help others?

Exam-style question

Outline three reasons why Muslims believe it is important to try to act to end the causes of crime. **(3 marks)**

Exam tip

Be clear in the three different reasons you offer and make sure you state them clearly.

Checkpoint

Strengthen

S1   What is the accepted understanding of a crime?

S2   What are the causes of crime and can you explain each one?

S3   What do individuals and organisations such as MCA and Mosaic do to tackle the causes of crime?

Challenge

C1   Why do you think that there is often a combination of factors that leads people to commit crime?

C2   How do you think ideas of justice may relate to offenders being released back into society?

C3   What do you think would be the hardest challenge for a Muslim who has committed a crime and been put in prison?

3.3 Good, evil and suffering

Learning objectives

- To understand Islamic teachings about good and evil.
- To understand Muslim beliefs about the nature of good and evil actions and how they are rewarded and punished.
- To explore Muslim beliefs and teachings about why people suffer.

Islamic beliefs about good, evil and suffering

Islam has a great deal to say about the ideas of good and evil. Good is seen to be things that have positive outcomes or help others. Evil is often understood to be things that are not good or things that hurt others. Evil can be further categorised into:

- **natural evil** – suffering caused by natural events not caused by humans, such as volcanic eruptions, floods or earthquakes
- **moral evil** – suffering that is directly caused by humans acting in a way that is considered morally wrong, such as bullying, murder, rape or terrorism.

Suffering is often seen to be a consequence of evil where a person undergoes physical, emotional or mental pain.

Many non-religious people use evidence such as the amount of suffering in the world or the fact that evil exists as arguments to suggest that God cannot be real. Muslims, however, believe that suffering has a purpose in life and that their teachings on good and evil lead those who follow them to be rewarded in the next life. Surah 76 in the Qur'an focuses on ideas of reward and punishment, with those who are followers of Allah being rewarded with Paradise, whilst those who turn away from Allah being punished.

Figure 3.6 Earthquakes, such as this in Haiti, are categorised as natural evils

Islamic teachings about good and evil

Islam teaches that:

- everyone is born with **fitrah**, the natural instinct to know the difference between good and evil. Muslims believe Allah gave humans free will and they must choose between following the teachings of Allah or turning away from him
- Allah ordered the Malaikah, or angels and **jinn**, spirits, to bow down before **Adam**, the first human. Iblis, one of the jinn, refused and said that he would forever tempt humans to choose wrong rather than right. Although Iblis is allowed to test humans, he is not equal to Allah and cannot hurt humans
- life on Earth is a period of testing where temptation is put in people's way. Muslims accept that people need to find their own solutions to resist temptation, and that their good and bad deeds will be judged before they can enter the afterlife
- Allah will forgive anyone who sincerely repents for their evil deeds since he is merciful

- everyone should try to follow the ideas of justice, mercy and forgiveness in their treatment of others and this is important for being rewarded in the next life.

Nature of good and evil actions

Muslims accept that behaving in a good way – for example, following the duties of Islam, praying to Allah and helping others – will allow Allah to see that they are trying to live their lives according to Islam and so they can be rewarded in the afterlife. Anyone who turns away from Allah and the messages given by his prophets or who fails to help others will be punished in the afterlife.

Many Muslims believe that this life on Earth is temporary and is a preparation for Akhirah, or life after death. They believe that on the Day of Judgement, Allah will judge them on the way they have lived their lives. If they have behaved correctly, Muslims believe they will go to al-Jannah. If not, they will be sent to Jahannam.

Non-religious attitudes on suffering

Many atheists see the existence of evil and suffering in the world as evidence that there is no God. This is often one of the strongest arguments to support rejection of religion and God. However, Muslims would consider that it is up to each individual to overcome such doubt and maintain their faith even when evidence challenges them to think otherwise.

Humanists do not commonly believe that evil or suffering are a punishment or due to any divine power. Because they do not believe in an afterlife, they therefore do not believe in the judgement of God or suffering as a result. Instead, they accept that humans make their own choices and must take responsibility for their actions. They also recognise that humans don't have control over natural occurrences such as volcanoes, floods or earthquakes but are aware that human influence on these matters can have both positive and negative impacts.

Islamic beliefs about suffering

Muslim beliefs about why humans suffer all relate in some form to the idea that part of being a Muslim is to submit to Allah and put faith in him. This means

Figure 3.7 Suffering

not challenging his authority or questioning why things such as evil and suffering happen. This is shown in Surah 21:23 in the Qur'an. This surah also suggests a connection between the ideas of suffering and the Day of Judgement, when all Muslims believe they will be judged by Allah on their deeds on Earth. They will be questioned about what they have done and it will be determined if they enter al-Jannah or Jahannam.

Some Islamic explanations for suffering follow, though different Muslims will consider some of these more important than others.

Sources of authority

He cannot be questioned for His acts, but they will be questioned (for theirs) (Surah 21:23)

Allah has a plan and suffering is part of this plan

One of the Six Key Beliefs for Muslims is al-Qadr or predestination. They believe that nothing happens without Allah allowing it, so their understanding of suffering is that it must be part of Allah's plan. Part of being a Muslim is submitting to Allah and accepting that there are some things about his plan and suffering that humans cannot understand. Suffering is a test of faith and character.

Sources of authority

Be sure We shall test you with something of fear and hunger, some loss in goods or lives or the fruits (of your toil), but give glad tidings to those who patiently persevere – Who say, when afflicted with calamity: To Allah we belong, and to Him is our return.
(Surah 2:155–156)

Muslims accept that Allah gave humans free will. Iblis tempts people to turn away from Allah and it is up to each person to choose whether or not to give in to this. Islam teaches that if a person chooses to act against the will of Allah, they will have to answer for that wrongdoing on the Day of Judgement.

Suffering is a reminder of sin and the revelation of Allah

Some Muslims believe that humans suffer on Earth because they deserve to as a result of sin. They have ignored the message of Allah and have become pre-occupied with their own selfish wants. Often Muslims may associate this with those who do not believe in Allah, as they think they have chosen to ignore the messages of the prophets and holy books as sources of authority.

Some forms of suffering are due to human action

Muslims accept that some forms of evil are not the result of Allah. Moral evil, such as actions caused directly by humans, is where humans choose to hurt others. Suffering, therefore, is not deserved and often innocent people can be hurt. This form of suffering is often difficult to understand as it is not the victim's fault.

Good can come from suffering

Muslims believe that Allah has a purpose for everything that happens and this includes suffering. Some Muslims believe that good can come out of suffering. It can help people cope with future suffering as it makes a person stronger and better able to deal with challenges. Furthermore, there are examples in life where suffering can have a positive outcome, such as childbirth.

Exam-style question

Explain two reasons why Muslims believe people suffer. **(4 marks)**

Exam tip

You have to give two different reasons to answer this question successfully. There are more than two reasons offered in this topic, so before you begin decide which ones you will include. Develop each explanation fully by using quotes and examples to support what you say.

Activities

1   Some types of suffering are difficult to categorise as natural or moral. Discuss with a partner how you would categorise these events. Would it be easy or difficult to accept the suffering in each case? Why?

 a A snowboarder dies in an avalanche triggered by a group of skiers showing off.
 b A man, who has never smoked in his life, dies of lung cancer.
 c A woman is self-conscious about her face because it was burned in an acid attack.

2   Make a list of actions that you think a Muslim should perform in order to be rewarded in Akhirah. Share your list with a friend to see if you agree. Once completed, create a list of things a Muslim should avoid in their lives to prevent them from going to Jahannam.

Summary

- Muslims believe the ideas of good, evil and suffering are directly related to each other.
- Muslims believe that all humans are born with the ability to understand the difference between good and evil.
- Muslims believe good actions will help them achieve their goal of al-Jannah in Akhirah, and evil actions will work to prevent it and lead them to Jahannam.
- Muslims accept there are various reasons to explain why humans suffer, including the belief that Allah has a plan and suffering is part of the plan.

Checkpoint

Strengthen

S1 What is the difference between natural and moral evil?
S2 Why are all Islamic explanations for why humans suffer linked to the Qur'an?
S3 What explanations do Muslims offer for why humans suffer?

Challenge

C1 Why do you think so many people use the existence of evil and suffering to argue that God cannot exist?
C2 What do you think Muslims can learn about suffering from the Prophet Muhammad?
C3 Why do you think people struggle to accept Islamic explanations for why suffering exists?

3.4 Punishment

Learning objectives

- To understand the nature of punishment and why punishment is important to Muslims.
- To explore Qur'anic teachings about punishment.
- To consider why punishment can be seen as justice and why punishment may be needed in society.

Punishment

In order for the law to work effectively, those who break the law must be punished. In the UK, laws are made by **Parliament** and enforced by the police. **Crimes** are judged in courts of law, which decide what punishment to impose. The nature of the punishment depends on the seriousness of the crime. The most common punishments given to offenders include fines, community service and imprisonment. In Islamic countries courts will refer to Shari'ah law in order to make legal decisions. Shari'ah law is the Islamic code of behaviour that is derived from the Qur'an and interpreted by leading Muslim scholars. It aims to help Muslims understand how they should lead every aspect of their lives according to the wishes of Allah. In terms of punishments for crimes, Shari'ah law divides offences into two general categories:

1 **Hadd** offences are serious crimes with set penalties. This includes crimes such as theft, where the set punishment is amputation of the offender's hand, and adultery, where the penalty is death by stoning. Other punishments may include caning, whipping or death.

2 **Tazir** offences are crimes for which the judge can decide what the punishment should be.

Sources of authority

O you who believe! The law of equality is prescribed to you in cases of murder: the free for the free, the slave for the slave, the woman for the woman. But if any remission is made by the brother of the slain, then grant any reasonable demand, and compensate him with handsome gratitude. This is a concession and a Mercy from your Lord. After this whoever exceeds the limits shall be in grave penalty. (Surah 2:178)

Sources of authority

The punishment of those who wage war against Allah and His Messenger, and strive with might and main for mischief through the land is: execution, or crucifixion, or the cutting off of hands and feet from opposite sides, or exile from the land: that is their disgrace in this world, and a heavy punishment is theirs in the Hereafter. (Surah 5:33)

Figure 3.8 A person being caned for a crime

Figure 3.9 The Qur'an

Why is punishment important to Muslims?

There is a lot of evidence in the Qur'an to show that punishment is a key idea supported in Islam. Punishment is important to Muslims.

- They believe Allah intended humans to build a society on Earth where every person lives in peace, justice and equality. Muslims believe that Allah sent messengers with this message, which is contained in the Qur'an.
- Muslims believe punishment for crimes is important because this will create a more stable society and prevent further crimes.
- Muslims believe that offenders need to be given the opportunity to change their behaviour and therefore punishment will allow them to do this. Muslims believe Allah is merciful and forgiving. The idea of Allah being forgiving is shown through one of his 99 names – al-Ghāfir, which means 'The forgiver.'
- The Qur'an teaches that punishment is important in Islam as it makes some amends for the crime committed.
- Muslims appear to follow some principles of the theory of situation ethics. This states that the action to be taken should suit the situation. So, for example, rather than simply judging the action of the crime, they take into account the reason behind the crime, such as being forced to steal due to poverty.

Some Muslims may be divided over their attitudes to punishment due to modern day society being so different to when sources of wisdom authority, such as the Qur'an, were originally written. As a result, some conflict may exist between the principles of Shari'ah law and the attitudes and laws of Western societies. Inevitably, this can lead to differences in opinion on how punishment should be applied, but the concept of punishment itself remains important to all Muslims.

How punishment can be justice

Punishment of an offender can be accepted to be a form of justice. The victim feels their crime has been dealt with if a suitable punishment is given to the offender. The punishment should be appropriate to the crime committed. In Islamic countries, punishments, such as the use of capital punishment, amputation and flogging, are often accepted under Islamic law. It would be seen that the offender has been appropriately punished for the crime they committed.

Sources of authority

Except for those who repent before they fall into your power: in that case, know that Allah is Oft-Forgiving, Most Merciful. (Surah 5:34)

But if the thief repents after his crime, and amends his conduct, Allah turns to him in forgiveness: for Allah is Oft-Forgiving, Most Merciful. (Surah 5:39)

Can you remember?

- What is justice and why is it important to Muslims?
- What do Muslims believe about the afterlife and how does this relate to ideas about punishment?
- What work is done by Muslim individuals and organisations to try to prevent the causes of crime?

Sources of authority

It was We Who revealed the Law (to Moses): therein was guidance and light. By its standard have been judged the Jews, by the prophets who bowed (as in Islam) to Allah's Will, by the rabbis and the doctors of law: for to them was entrusted the protection of Allah's Book, and they were witnesses thereto: therefore fear not men, but fear Me, and sell not My Signs for a miserable price. If any do fail to judge by (the light of) what Allah has revealed, they are (no better than) Unbelievers. We ordained therein for them: "Life for life, eye for eye, nose for nose, ear for ear, tooth for tooth, and wounds equal for equal." But if any one remits the retaliation by way of charity, it is an act of atonement for himself. And if any fail to judge by (the light of) what Allah has revealed, they are (no better than) wrong-doers. And in their footsteps We sent Jesus the son of Mary, confirming the Law that had come before him: We sent him the Gospel: therein was guidance and light, and confirmation of the Law that had come before him: a guidance and an admonition to those who fear Allah. (Surah 5:44-46)

Why is punishment needed in society?

Muslims believe punishment is needed in society for a number of reasons.

- It maintains law and order and protects the people living in a country. This is important to Muslims as they believe Allah wants a just society.
- It sets expected examples of behaviour and allows people to live their lives within these limits.
- It gives offenders the opportunity to reflect on their actions and change their behaviours. Muslims believe in reconciliation and giving offenders a chance to rehabilitate.
- It allows victims of crime to feel safe and may deter others from crime.
- It makes the offenders realise their impact on the lives of others. Muslims believe that how they live their lives on Earth will determine their afterlife. They accept that all humans will be judged by Allah on the Day of Judgement when it will be decided whether they go to al-Jannah or Jahannam.

Exam tip

This question focuses on teachings so you need to make sure these are explained in your answer. Examiners will award one mark for stating each teaching and then a second mark for explaining it more fully. You need to offer two different teachings in order to achieve the full marks available.

Activities ?

1 Write a response to the following, making sure you explain your reasons fully:

   a Why do you think a Muslim will be very careful in their everyday lives to consider every action they do?

   b Do you think the idea that Allah is watching is enough to prevent Muslims from committing crimes? Why or why not?

2 With a partner, make a list of the pros and cons of having punishments in society. After your list is completed, share your thoughts with others. Take a vote on whether you think having punishments are a good or bad thing in society.

Exam-style question

Explain two teachings of the Qur'an about punishment. **(4 marks)**

Summary

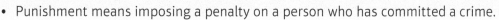

- Punishment means imposing a penalty on a person who has committed a crime.
- Shari'ah Law is the code of behaviour used by Muslims, especially in Islamic countries, which is consulted on legal matters.
- Punishment is important to Muslims because they believe it creates a stable society, it is fair and just, and it is prescribed by Allah.
- The Qur'an provides teachings and guidance on punishments.
- Punishment can be seen as a form of justice and is needed in society.

Checkpoint

Strengthen

S1 What is punishment?

S2 What does the Qur'an teach about punishment and why is punishment important?

S3 Why can punishment be seen as a form of justice?

Challenge

C1 Do you think it matters that punishments for the same crimes may differ between different countries?

C2 Why do you think some people may not agree with punishments used in some Islamic countries?

C3 Do you think punishments are always just and fair?

3.5 The aims of punishment

Learning objectives

- To understand what the aims of punishment are and the Muslim response to them.
- To consider the strengths and weaknesses of each of the aims of punishment.
- To explore Qur'anic teachings about punishment.

What are the aims of punishment?

There are a number of key aims that the law hopes to achieve through imposing punishments on those who commit crimes.

Figure 3.10 The aims of punishment

Protection
To protect society from criminals. Means protecting victims of crimes that have already been committed, and the rest of society. Dangerous criminals who have committed awful crimes can be locked up away from society to offer this protection.

Retribution
Criminals should 'pay' for their crimes. It can help victims feel a sense of justice that the offender was punished. Retribution involves the offender losing something, e.g. freedom if imprisoned, or time if given community service. It could be a fine where the money may be used to help compensate the victim.

Aims of punishment

Deterrence
This means to discourage people from committing crimes. If a person sees how someone has been punished for a crime, the idea is they will not want to suffer the same punishment and therefore will not commit the same crime.

Reformation
Punishments are intended to help the offender see that what they have done is wrong and to give them the opportunity to reform and change. Reformation can involve providing the offender with education, skills, qualifications or job training so they can become a law-abiding citizen again.

Aim of punishment	Strengths	Weaknesses
Protection	• Victims will feel safe from criminals. • Other people in society are safe from becoming victims of crime committed by that offender.	• The protection is only relevant while the offender is in prison. When they are released they could re offend. • Sometimes prison sentences seem lenient. This may mean an offender doesn't spend long in prison and the protection is limited.
Retribution	• Makes the victim of a crime feel a sense of justice; that the offender 'got what they deserved'. • The offender is 'made to pay', which could be enough to make them change their ways.	• Doesn't always work. Some victims feel that the punishment isn't severe enough. • Often many offenders commit the same offence again, meaning the punishment has had little effect.
Deterrence	• The punishment will hopefully be enough to prevent others committing the same crimes.	• Doesn't always work. Nearly half of all criminals re offend and prisons are full.
Reformation	• Gives offenders an opportunity to change their lives and make amends for what they have done wrong. • Can often involve skills development or training, which means the offender has more opportunities available to them in the future.	• Sometimes seems like the criminal is being given a fresh chance rather than a punishment. • Some could feel the offender has benefited rather than punished. Victims could feel they have not had justice.

Table 3.1 Strengths and weaknesses of each aim of punishment

Muslim attitudes

Muslims believe that the aims of punishment are important, though as individual Muslims may consider different aims to be more important. As the Qur'anic passages in the Sources of authority boxes show, there is evidence for ideas of punishment providing protection for society, a deterrent for other offenders, reformation of the offender and retribution for the victim. Muslims accept that the law of the country is important and needs to be followed by all citizens. This will hopefully help to create a peaceful and just society – key ideas within Islam. Muslims also believe that judgement is important and although it is not a human's place to judge others, the law has to be followed and when it is not, suitable punishments should be given.

Qur'anic teachings about punishment

The Qur'an carries many teachings related to the aims of punishment. Shari'ah law, which is the legal system used in many Islamic countries, is derived from the Qur'an, showing the important role it has.

Muslims believe Allah intended for humans to build a society on Earth where every human lives in peace, justice and equality. Punishment is important in trying to establish this.

- Muslims believe it is important that society is protected from dangerous offenders. Innocent citizens should feel safe within society and punishments should be sufficient for crimes committed in order that society is protected. This is one of the key aims of punishment in the UK, which is also recognised as important by Muslims. The other aims of punishment are understood through this key idea.
- Muslims believe retribution for crimes is important because this means the offender is made to pay for their crime, which in turn will create a more stable society and prevent further crimes.
- The Qur'an teaches that punishment is important in Islam as it is recompense for the crime committed. Muslims recognise that if a person has done wrong, they should be punished. Furthermore, Muslims believe that although they must obey the rules of the country in which they live, Allah also sees everything and therefore knows when a person does wrong. Muslims believe this will be taken into account on the Day of Judgement.
- Deterrence is a key aim of punishment seen within Islam. Shari'ah punishments focus on public and often humiliating displays of punishment. Punishments such as stoning take place in front of crowds and persistent thieves can have their hands cut off, to try to encourage others not to commit the same crimes. There are 37 verses in the Qur'an that speak about exemplary punishments.
- Muslims believe that offenders need to be given the opportunity to change their behaviour and reform themselves. Muslims believe Allah is merciful and forgiving – key ideas shown in the characteristics of Allah demonstrated within his 99 names. Surah 4: 26-32 also talks about the forgiving nature of Allah and the fact he knows everything a person does. Muslims believe that a person should pay for their crimes and hopefully then be given forgiveness. Muslims accept that Allah wants offenders to understand that their behaviour was wrong and that punishment should allow this and provide the opportunity for them to alter their ways. The Qur'an focuses on this in Surah 5:39.

Sources of authority

Allah does wish to make clear to you and to show you the ordinances of those before you; and (He does wish to) turn to you (in Mercy): and Allah is All-Knowing, All-Wise. Allah does wish to turn to you, but the wish of those who follow their lusts is that you should turn away (from Him),—far, far away. Allah does wish to lighten your (difficulties): for man was created weak (in flesh). (Surah 4:26–28)

Sources of authority

The punishment of those who wage war against Allah and His Messenger, and strive with might and main for mischief through the land is: execution, or crucifixion, or the cutting off of hands and feet from opposite sides, or exile from the land: that is their disgrace in this world, and a heavy punishment is theirs in the Hereafter. (Surah 5:33)

Sources of authority

But if the thief repents after his crime, and amends his conduct, Allah turns to him in forgiveness: for Allah is Oft-forgiving, Most Merciful. (Surah 5:39)

Activities ?

1   Rank the aims of punishment in order from what you think is most to least effective. Explain why you have put them in this order. Share your thoughts with a partner. Do they agree with you? Why or why not?

2   Write a speech giving your own opinion on the following statement. 'Islamic punishments are too severe in today's society; imprisonment is enough.' Make sure you refer to the aims of punishment and their strengths and weaknesses in your speech, explaining your ideas fully.

3   Copy out each of the quotes from the Qur'an about punishment. Outline what you think each one is saying. Identify any links to the four aims of punishment.

Exam-style question

Explain two reasons why punishment is important to Muslims. In your answer you must refer to a source of wisdom and authority. **(5 marks)**

Exam tip

You need to offer two different reasons why the idea of punishment is important to Muslims. To achieve the final mark you need to refer to a source of authority or wisdom so consider carefully what quote you could include to support.

Extend your knowledge

Shari'ah law has been at the centre of many debates concerning issues of crime and punishment. Some Islamic countries who are ruled solely according to Islamic principles enforce the teachings and guidance of Shari'ah law. Shari'ah is literally interpreted to mean 'path' and in essence guides all aspects of Muslim life: daily routines, family and religious obligations and criminal matters, as well as financial dealings. Muhammad died in 632 CE and Shari'ah law was compiled based on teachings in the Qur'an and Hadith after his death. At this time, it went through a number of developments before it was finalised and even today, differences may be seen within its implementation for Sunni and Shi'a Muslims. In reality, issues of crime and punishment are controversial and many Islamic countries choose to recognise Shari'ah law but may not necessarily practically apply all the rulings, feeling that lesser punishments sometimes are sufficient in today's society.

Summary

- There are four main recognised aims of punishment: reformation, deterrence, retribution and protection.
- There are various strengths and weaknesses of each aim of punishment.
- Muslims believe punishment is important and support the aims of punishment.
- The Qur'an contains guidance on why punishment is important.
- Shari'ah law is used by Muslims to decide punishment in some situations and it demonstrates the aims of punishment through its guidance.

Checkpoint

Strengthen

S1 What are the four aims of punishment?

S2 What are the strengths and weaknesses of each aim of punishment?

S3 What does the Qur'an say about the aims of punishment?

Challenge

C1 Why might some people say the aims of punishment are not always achieved?

C2 Why might some people argue that punishments need to be tougher in today's society?

C3 Why do some Islamic punishments seem extreme in comparison to those given in the UK?

3.6 Forgiveness

Learning objectives

- To understand the nature of forgiveness.
- To consider how offenders are forgiven by the community and why this is needed.
- To consider the nature of restorative justice and why it is important for criminals.

Forgiveness

Figure 3.11 Forgiveness

Forgiveness is the action or process of forgiving someone, accepting that they are sorry for their actions and moving on from what has happened. Forgiveness is often linked with the idea of **reconciliation**, which means to make up after an argument. Peace is the outcome of a situation where forgiveness and reconciliation are applied.

Muslim teachings about forgiveness

Muslims believe that conflicts should always be resolved using the ideas of forgiveness and reconciliation. Muslims hold certain beliefs and teachings about these ideas:

- Islam teaches that Allah is merciful and forgiving. One name given to Allah is 'the **compassionate** and merciful' showing Allah forgives people and Muslims believe they should try to do this too.
- Muslims believe that if a person is truly sorry and **repents** for what they have done wrong, then forgiveness should be shown.

Sources of authority

O you who believe! The law of equality is prescribed to you in cases of murder: the free for the free, the slave for the slave, the woman for the woman. But if any remission is made by the brother of the slain, then grant any reasonable demand, and compensate him with handsome gratitude; this is a concession and a Mercy from your Lord. After this whoever exceeds the limits shall be in grave penalty. (Surah 2:178)

Sources of authority

… but if a person forgives and makes reconciliation, his reward is due from Allah… (Surah 42:40)

Say: 'O my servants who have transgressed against their souls! Despair not of the Mercy of Allah: for Allah forgives all sins: for He is Oft-Forgiving, Most Merciful. (Surah 39:53)

Sources of authority

O you who believe! Truly, among your wives and your children are (some that are) enemies to yourselves: so beware of them! But if you forgive and overlook, and cover up (their faults), verily Allah is Oft-Forgiving, Most Merciful. (Surah 64:14)

Figure 3.12 Restorative justice

- Muhammad taught that people should try to forgive those who have wronged them or offended them.
- Islam is a religion of peace and submission to Allah, and ideas of forgiveness support this.
- There are examples in the Qur'an where it says that a life can be taken for a life, supporting the use of capital punishment. However, it also says that if a killer is forgiven by the victim's family and can pay compensation to the family, their life can be spared.
- There are some actions in Islam that display examples of forgiveness: Hajj is one of these. During Hajj Muslims stand on Mount Arafat and ask for forgiveness from Allah. Hajj is the fifth Pillar of Islam and a duty for Muslims to complete once in their lifetime. Muslims believe that through enduring this difficult pilgrimage and repenting for their sins, Allah will forgive them, showing how important forgiveness is.
- Muslims believe that on the Day of Judgement, they will stand in front of Allah and be judged on their actions on Earth. Muslims believe that if a person is truly sorry and repents for their sins, Allah will forgive them.

Community responses and restorative justice

In order for an offender to realise the impact of their actions on others and change their ways, it is important that forgiveness happens. This is not always possible, especially for the worst crimes, but Muslims recognise the importance of trying to forgive those who do wrong. Some criminals who have spent a short period of time in prison or those not seen as dangerous to society may complete a period of community service. This is intended to be retribution, where offenders can make amends to the community and any victims of their crime for what they did.

This is essential to allow everyone involved to be able to move on with their lives. If the action committed by the offender was against the community, such as anti-social behaviour, graffiti, or similar crimes, the action of reconciling with the community can help to ease tensions. The community may feel as though they have had justice as they have seen the offender pay for their crime. The offender will be able to see the positive impact they could have on the community and society if they try. The ummah, or community, is a key idea within Islam. Muslims believe that they should do all they can to protect the ummah and ensure people live in harmony with each other.

Restorative justice is a recognised system now used with offenders to help them understand the impact their actions have had on victims, their families and the wider community. The offender and victim of the crime can speak and share their thoughts and this will hopefully lead to reconciliation, where relationships can be restored. Restorative justice is a reasonable idea within Islam and complements traditional Islamic teachings of peace, forgiveness and justice.

Activities

1 Write down three examples of things that you could forgive and three examples of things you could not forgive. Explain to a partner why you would or would not be able to forgive in these situations.

2 Write a conversation to show the idea of restorative justice between a victim, their family and an offender; the offender was found guilty of theft and took items from the victim's house. What do you think each person would say to each other? How do you think the others would respond? Act out your conversation as a role play for the class to discuss.

3 Write a response to the following statement: 'We should always forgive and forget. Consider arguments on both sides in your answer.

Can you remember?

- Why is justice important to Muslims and how is this related to ideas about forgiveness?
- What does Islam teach about good and evil and why some people suffer?
- What do Muslims believe about Allah and how this relates to ideas of forgiveness?

Exam-style questions

Explain two reasons why forgiveness is so important to Muslims. In your answer you must refer to a source of wisdom or authority. **(5 marks)**

Exam tip

Take each point you want to explain separately, and fully develop it using examples to show what you mean and explaining each idea fully. Try to use some quotes from the Qur'an where relevant. When you have completed one idea, move onto the next one. Remember that you also need to include reference to a source of authority or wisdom in your answer such as the Qur'an or Hadith.

Summary

- Islam teaches that forgiveness and reconciliation are important after conflict, including in situations where crimes have been committed.
- Muslims believe that Allah is forgiving, merciful and compassionate and that they should try to be too.
- The Qur'an gives examples of forgiveness, showing it is important.
- Restorative justice is compatible with ideas within Islam.
- Muslims believe forgiveness is important both for the victim and the offender.

Checkpoint

Strengthen

S1 What is forgiveness?

S2 What do Muslims believe about forgiveness?

S3 What is restorative justice and how is this important in Islam?

Challenge

C1 Why might it be hard sometimes to forgive others and move on?

C2 Where might Muslims look if they need advice and guidance on issues associated with forgiveness?

C3 Why do you think some people may have doubts about the positive outcome of restorative justice?

3.7 The treatment of criminals

Learning objectives

- To understand what Muslims believe about how criminals should be treated.
- To consider attitudes towards the treatment of criminals.

Figure 3.13 A person being tortured

Muslim teachings about the treatment of criminals

Islam is a religion of peace that promotes ideas of justice and forgiveness. However, many Muslims do support severe punishments, such as caning and capital punishment. They believe it has a role and purpose in terms of preventing further crimes, and allows a victim to receive full retribution.

Although Muslims support the use of punishments, including some that are viewed by others as more severe, they also believe how criminals should be treated fairly while waiting for their trial, once they have been convicted and when they are punished. The Qur'an reinforces the fair treatment of criminals when it mentions them distinctly in terms of their treatment, as depicted in Surah 76:8.

However, Muslims may interpret passages of the Qur'an differently. For example, some Muslims believe Surah 76:1–12 teaches us to be merciful towards prisoners and treat them with respect, while others may hold that someone who has committed a crime should face suitable punishment and therefore their rights should not be upheld in the same way.

Sources of authority

And they feed, for the love of Allah, the indigent, the orphan, and the captive… (Surah 76:8)

Use of torture

Torture is when a person is threatened and severely hurt in order to extract information, or it is to punish someone or to get revenge for something they are believed to have done.

Although there are examples in the Qur'an that suggest that Islam supports the use of torture, the majority of Muslims today would suggest it is not right to torture a prisoner or possible offender. They believe that everyone was created by Allah and therefore deserves respect. In the time of Muhammad, there are suggestions that torture was sanctioned for the purposes of interrogation and the Qur'an does appear to suggest that severe forms of punishment involving pain and suffering could be used. Muslim principles are sometimes seen to be in line with ethical theories, such as situation ethics. This is based on the theory that the resulting action is based on what is best for the individual situation and therefore universal laws cannot be applied in the same way. This could be seen to authorise some forms of torture, as it may

Figure 3.14 Every person should be entitled to basic human rights

Sources of authority

The punishment of those who wage war against Allah and His Messenger, and strive with might and main for mischief through the land is: execution, or crucifixion, or the cutting off of hands and feet from opposite sides… (Surah 5:33)

be the best action in ensuring that other people are saved or that human life is prioritised. This theory could also apply if the best possible outcome is the use of torture for the benefit of the greater good.

Human rights

Human rights are the fundamental rights that all humans are entitled to, whatever their age, gender, race, colour, nationality or where they live. This includes basic necessities, such as water, food and shelter, as well as the right to a fair trial in cases of crime, and the right to justice and equality. Muslim principles are seen to be in favour of human rights. When it comes to the treatment of prisoners, most Muslims believe that human rights should be upheld and it is important that a person accused of a crime has a fair trial and justice is applied. Muslims believe all humans were created by Allah and they accept that all life is sacred and special. Some Muslims, however, may accept that if a person has committed a crime they should have to pay a suitable consequence. This may lead them to consider the idea of situations where rights are taken away and, although they recognise life is special, accept that a person should be punished.

Leading on from ideas that Muslims believe prisoners should have human rights, one of these rights includes the right to a fair trial. Muslims think this is important because a person should be considered innocent until they are proven guilty. Their human rights mean they should have fair representation as well as the right to put forward their account of events. Islam teaches that justice is important both for the victim of a crime and the person accused of committing it. It must be proven that a person committed a crime before a punishment is set.

Trial by jury

Muslims believe in justice and equality. In many courts in the UK, a judge presides over the events when a case is brought. However, it is a jury of peers of the accused who will listen to the evidence and come to a verdict. By having a group of people making this decision, there is likely to be less bias and it means the right to a fair trial is upheld. Muslims support trial by jury for prisoners in order to ensure justice is shown. Some Muslims, in cases where Shari'ah law is applied, may accept that a trial by jury is not required as it is clear a crime has been committed and the appropriate punishment should be given.

Atheist and Humanist attitudes towards the treatment of criminals

Atheists and **Humanists** are united in their views that human rights are of paramount importance. They do not hold any religious beliefs but many ideas seen within religions are present. For example, Humanists teach that you should 'treat others as you would like to be treated' and this is a key principle seen within every religion, including Islam.

Atheists and Humanists advocate that prisoners should be treated fairly and with justice. This involves them being cared for appropriately if detained, for example, they shouldn't face any form of torture. Prisoners also have the right to a fair and unbiased trial. Decisions such as how to treat criminals who have committed crimes

Figure 3.15 The right to a fair trial

Sources of authority

Allah commands justice, the doing of good, and liberality to kith and kin, and He forbids all shameful deeds, and injustice and rebellion: He instructs you, that you may receive admonition (Surah 16:90)

No Arab has any superiority over a non-Arab, nor does a non-Arab have any superiority over an Arab. Nor does a white man have any superiority over a black man, or the black man any superiority over the white man. You are all the children of Adam, and Adam was created from clay.

(Prophet Muhammad's last sermon)

Figure 3.16 Trial by jury

are difficult for all people – religious believers and non-religious people alike. This is because no two situations are exactly the same. For religious believers such as Muslims, they may refer to sources of authority such as the Qur'an or an example of Muhammad in order to decide what the correct course of action should be. However, in some situations, a person's individual conscience may also be important in determining what is right and wrong, making ethical decisions difficult.

Activities ?

1. Imagine you are in charge of the care of a group of prisoners. What things would you need to consider to ensure they are treated fairly? Make a list of ideas. How would you ensure these things were carried out so the prisoners were treated in an acceptable way?
2. Write a letter to your local MP trying to persuade them that prisoners deserve rights too. Give examples of the things you think they are entitled to, offering reasons for your view.
3. Consider the following statement and create a table of arguments that agree and disagree with it: 'Prisoners should always be treated with respect.' What might a Muslim say about this statement and why?

Exam-style question

In this question, 3 of the marks awarded will be for your spelling, punctuation and grammar and your use of specialist terminology.

'Criminals deserve to be treated fairly and justly.' Evaluate this statement considering arguments for and against. In your response you should

- refer to Muslim teachings
- reach a justified conclusion.
(12 marks)

Exam tip

It is worth taking time to think about this statement carefully before you begin writing your answer. When you write your opinion, make sure your answer considers a range of different views, including what a Muslim would say. Level descriptors are used to award marks for this style of question so bear this in mind. Also remember that to achieve the top marks, you need to consider a range of views and reasons and then offer a conclusion with evidence.

Summary

- Islam is a religion of peace and justice.
- Muslims believe that the treatment of prisoners in a fair and just way is important.
- Most Muslims do not accept torture of prisoners today.
- Muslims believe prisoners are entitled to human rights and a fair trial.
- Atheists and Humanists hold similar views to Muslims, although they justify their views using different reasons.
- Atheists and Humanists are supporters of human rights and the fair treatment of all prisoners.

Checkpoint

Strengthen

S1 Why do Muslims not support the use of torture against prisoners?
S2 Why are human rights important to Muslims?
S3 What would an atheist or Humanist say about the treatment of prisoners?

Challenge

C1 Why do you think Muslims may hold different views about an issue like the torture of prisoners?
C2 Where do you think a Muslim would go for advice on how prisoners should be treated today?
C3 Why do you think atheist and Humanist views are becoming more popular with people today?

3.8 Capital punishment

Learning objectives

- To understand the nature and purpose of capital punishment.
- To consider Muslim teachings about capital punishment, including reasons why some Muslims would support it and others would not.
- To understand atheist and Humanist attitudes towards the death penalty.

The nature and purpose of capital punishment

Figure 3.17 Scaffold

Capital punishment is also known as the death penalty. It is when a person is executed using a country's legal procedures for a serious crime that they have been found guilty of committing. The death penalty was abolished in Great Britain in 1965 and Northern Ireland in 1973 for all crimes except treason, and was abolished completely in 1998. Other nations in the world, including some states in the USA and some Islamic nations, such as Iran and Saudi Arabia, still allow the death penalty. Methods of execution include hanging, lethal injection, the electric chair, beheading and firing squad.

The purposes of capital punishment are included below.

- **Retribution** This is the idea that if a person is guilty of a crime, they deserve to be punished in proportion to the seriousness of their crime. Part of the purpose of capital punishment is that if a person has committed the most serious crime of murder, a suitable punishment, and therefore the allocation of justice, would be for them to lose their life.

- **Repentance** When a person faces the death penalty it means their life will be taken and they will not be rehabilitated or return to society. But, it is hoped that they will face up to what they have done and take the time before the death penalty is carried out to repent and express remorse. Muslims believe this is important as they accept that Allah is merciful and forgives those who are sorry and repent for what they have done wrong.

- **Closure for the victim's family** The use of capital punishment in crimes such as murder may bring some relief to the family of the victim. It may bring their suffering to an end and hopefully allow them to move on with their lives, although obviously without their loved one. It will also hopefully allow them to feel that they have received justice because the offender has been punished.

- **Prevention of re offending** One effect of capital punishment is that it prevents the offender from being released into society and committing the same act again. It can almost be seen as protecting society from them.

- **Deterrent** The use of capital punishment is believed to act as a deterrent for other people who might think of committing the same crime. Once they realise the consequence of the crime, the hope is that they would not commit the same act because they would not want to suffer the same fate.

Muslim beliefs and teachings

Islam is, in principle, in favour of the death penalty for some crimes although there are a small number of Muslims who are in favour of abolishing it. This is mainly because the Qur'an indicates that the death penalty can be used for certain crimes such as murder, rape, homosexual acts and **apostasy** (someone working against Islam). However, the Qur'an also states that the use of capital punishment is not compulsory and not the only option available for the punishment of offenders. Other prominent ideas within Islam are those of forgiveness and peace, which would suggest that capital punishment is wrong.

Sources of authority

…take not life, which Allah has made sacred, except by way of justice and law: thus doth He command you, that you may learn wisdom. (Surah 6:151)

On that account: We ordained for the Children of Israel that is anyone slew a person – unless it be for murder or for spreading mischief in the land – it would be as if he slew the whole people: and if anyone saved a life, it would be as if he saved the life of the whole people… (Surah 5:32)

Why would Muslims support capital punishment?

They might support it because:

- the Qur'an says the death penalty can be used for some crimes
- Shari'ah law agrees with the Qur'an and in countries where Shar'iah law is used, the death penalty can be used
- there are examples where the death penalty is seen to have been commanded for certain actions
- According to the Qur'an, the death penalty can only be used as a last resort, which removes the concern of some that innocent people could be put to death
- Muhammad made statements suggesting he agreed with the death penalty. When Muhammad was the ruler of Medina, he sentenced people to death for committing murder.

Sources of authority

Abdullah (b. Mas'ud) reported Allah's Messenger (Peace be upon him) as saying: It is not permissible to take the life of a Muslim who bears testimony (to the fact that there is no god but Allah, and I am the Messenger of Allah), but in one of the three cases: the married adulterer, a life for life, and the deserter of his Din (Islam), abandoning the community.

(Hadith – Sahih Muslim 16:4152)

Why do some Muslims not support capital punishment?

Some Muslims may oppose the use of the death penalty for the reasons given below.

> Why do we **kill** people who **kill** people to show **kill**ing people is wrong?

Figure 3.18 Opposing the death penalty

- The scholars of Shari'ah law do not agree on the rules of how and when the death penalty should be used, so some Muslims feel it may not be applied fairly.
- The Qur'an puts the death penalty forward as one option that can be used for punishment but Muslims also believe in the sanctity of life, peace and forgiveness which are seen to conflict with the death penalty.
- Some Muslims may use non-religious arguments and be concerned about putting innocent people to death. Others feel that by taking the life of another means you are no better than the offender.

Non-religious attitudes

Humanists and other atheists generally oppose the use of the death penalty because:

- they believe premeditated killing is wrong, even when carried out by the state
- they uphold the regard for human life being special, which is part of the Universal Declaration of Human Rights
- they believe there is the possibility of error and someone who is innocent could end up being executed
- they think that the use of the death penalty means the criminal escapes rather than receiving justice.
- they do not refer to any higher power or 'God' so believe that there is no afterlife and no form of judgement.

Some may believe that when ethical theories, such as situation ethics, are applied to an individual situation that there are times when capital punishment could be seen as the better action, even if they would normally oppose capital punishment. An example of this would be if it prevented further loss of human life and upheld ideas of justice. Some Muslims may also be opposed to the ideas above in varying ways, with some agreeing that capital punishment is always wrong, while others might consider its application only necessary in particular circumstances.

Activities **?**

1. Consider each of the following statements and make a list of arguments for and against each one. Make sure you include some Islamic arguments. Share your arguments with a partner before you write your own opinion on each statement.

   a. 'If one person murders another, they should always face the death penalty.'

   b. 'Capital punishment is an effective deterrent against murder.'

   c. 'Someone who is spared the death penalty should pay compensation to the family of their victim.'

2. Read each of the quotes in the Sources of authority boxes. In your own words, explain what each one is saying. Do they support or go against the idea of the use of capital punishment?

3. Imagine you have been asked to write a letter to the Prime Minister to support the death penalty being brought back to the UK for the most serious crimes. What would you put in your letter? What arguments would you use? Write your letter and read it aloud to the class. Vote on how persuasive each other's letters are.

Exam-style question

In this question, 3 of the marks awarded will be for your spelling, punctuation and grammar and your use of specialist terminology. 'Muslims should always support the use of the death penalty.' Evaluate this statement, considering arguments for and against. In your response you should

- refer to Muslim teachings
- reach a justified conclusion.

(12 marks)

Exam tip

This statement is about the controversial topic of capital punishment. You need to show awareness of why it is controversial in your answer. Remember that not all Muslims hold the same beliefs about this topic so your answer needs to demonstrate this. Make sure you develop each argument you include and use effective and well-argued reasons to support each viewpoint.

Can you remember?

- What do Muslims teach about judgement, punishment and reward?
- Why do Muslims believe life is special and sacred?
- Why do Muslims believe forgiveness is important?

Summary

- Capital punishment is used in some Islamic countries that follow Shari'ah law.
- The purposes of capital punishment include retribution, repentance, closure for the victim's family, protection of society and deterrence.
- Not all Muslims support the use of capital punishment.
- The Qur'an suggests that there are other options for the punishment of serious crimes.
- Atheists and Humanists do not support the death penalty.

Checkpoint

Strengthen

S1 What is capital punishment?

S2 What does the Qur'an say about capital punishment and how might this be used by some Muslims?

S3 What reasons might some Muslims give for not supporting the use of capital punishment?

Challenge

C1 How might a Muslim's view about the death penalty be based on their beliefs about life after death?

C2 Why can Islamic views about justice and forgiveness be seen to be in conflict with each other when applied to ideas about the death penalty?

C3 Do you think it matters if people hold different views about an issue such as capital punishment?

Recap: Crime and punishment

Use the activities and exam-style questions on the following pages to reinforce your learning before you move on to the next chapter.

Recall quiz

Crime and justice

1   What is justice?
2   Why is justice important for Muslims?
3   How is justice shown through the Six Beliefs of Islam for Sunni Muslims and the five roots of 'Usul ad-Din for Shi'a Muslims?
4   How are ideas of peace, justice and forgiveness shown in actions such as the Five Pillars of Islam?
5   How do issues surrounding al-Qadr relate to the issue of crime?
6   Why is the Day of Judgement so important to Muslims?

Action to end the causes of crime

7   What are the causes of crime?
8   Which Muslim organisations have tried to take action to end the causes of crime?

Good, evil and suffering

9   What is a good action for a Muslim?
10 What is a bad action for a Muslim?
11 What is suffering?
12 What are the two types of evil and suffering?
13 Why do Muslims believe humans suffer?
14 How are ideas about jihad related to the issues of crime and punishment?
15 How is Islam a 'way of life' and how does this affect Muslim beliefs about topics such as crime and punishment?
16 Why do Muslims try to avoid actions associated with crime?

Punishment

17 What is punishment?
18 How is punishment a form of justice?

The aims of punishment

19 What are the four aims of punishment?

Forgiveness

20 What is forgiveness?
21 Why is forgiveness important to Muslims?
22 What is restorative justice?
23 Why is restorative justice important for the victim and offender?
24 How are ideas about the Akhirah connected to the theme of crime and punishment?

The treatment of criminals

25 How do Muslims believe prisoners should be treated?
26 How do sources of authority, such as holy books and prophets, help Muslims facing issues concerning crime and punishment?

Capital punishment

27 What is capital punishment?
28 What do Muslims believe about capital punishment?
29 How do ideas about Allah influence Muslim beliefs about crime and punishment?

Activities ?

1 Create a list of any new terms you have learned in this unit. Practise your knowledge of them by creating a set of flashcards and testing yourself about your knowledge.

2 Consider the following statements and write a response, giving your own opinion:

   a 'Crime and punishment is a growing problem in society today.'

   b 'Punishments for the most severe crimes deserve capital punishment.'

   c 'Justice doesn't make a person feel better.'

   d 'God doesn't forgive people – only the person who has been wronged can do this.'

3 Create a mind map showing the new knowledge you have gained in this chapter. Use colour and pictures to help you learn the information.

4 As a group, create a series of scenarios that you can act out to the class to generate discussion and debate about the topics in this chapter. Try to prepare some questions to focus the discussion at the end.

Exam questions

- Outline three reasons why Muslims try to forgive. **(3 marks)**

- Explain two aims of punishment. **(4 marks)**

- Explain two Muslims teachings about justice. In your answer you must refer to a source of wisdom or authority. **(5 marks)**

- In this question, 3 of the marks awarded will be for your spelling, punctuation and grammar and your use of specialist terminology. 'There is no acceptable reason to explain why humans suffer.' Evaluate this statement, considering arguments for and against. In your response you should

   ◦ refer to Muslim teachings

   ◦ reach a justified conclusion.

(12 marks)

Exam tips

- Make sure you understand the demands of each question. Think carefully about what you are being asked to include in your answer.

- The last two questions have more marks available so you need to take more time with these questions. Make sure you develop each point you make fully and support each reason or argument you present with relevant evidence and examples.

- Make sure you check through your answers carefully once complete, to ensure you eliminate any silly errors.

- When presenting an argument, make sure you have prepared each of your arguments fully by having evidence and quotes to support the points you want to make.

- When using different formats (e.g. letter, email), make sure you apply the correct style of writing. If you are trying to persuade someone of your view, consider what questions they may ask you or points they may challenge you about in order to present a strong and focused argument.

Extend: Crime and punishment

Source

'Should it be brought back?'

A debate has opened up again today after the case of Rasul Al-Rahim was heard in court. Rasul is standing trial for the murders of an entire family. It was alleged that on Monday 16th June, Rasul broke into the house of the Lewis family and killed them. The Lewis family – father Sam, mother Jane and children Claire (7) and William (5) – didn't stand a chance. Rasul used a knife he took from the kitchen and stabbed the family, who could do little to defend themselves. His defence in court was that he didn't mean to do it as they weren't supposed to be home. All he wanted was to steal their belongings and it all went wrong. It was a case of wrong time, wrong place as the Lewis family were supposed to be out, but because William wasn't feeling well, they had decided to return home early.

The debate about whether capital punishment should be brought back has come around again as a result of this case. Those in favour argue that this was a severe and horrific crime, where only the harshest punishment possible should be applied. Rasul, a Muslim, failed to show any true remorse for his crime in court and at the beginning of the trial seemed to be enjoying proceedings as he was the centre of attention. As the trial progressed, however, and perhaps the seriousness of the occasion became more apparent, he seemed to change. The Muslim chaplain from the prison where he was kept on remand until the trial came to court to offer support. He has worked with Rasul in prison to try to make him see that what he did was wrong and to prepare him to accept that he will be facing a strong punishment. He has also spoken to Rasul about what he can possibly do with his time in prison to change his life and start to make amends for what he did, looking at educational choices available to him. The issue of punishment within Islam has been mentioned. If Rasul was tried for this crime in his home country of Iran, it is entirely possible to suggest that he would now be facing the death penalty since Iran bases its laws on Shari'ah law. The jury convicted Rasul and he is now awaiting sentence. As it is a case tried in the UK, the judge will assess the crime and in tomorrow's final hearing, probably hand down a life sentence to Rasul, with no chance of parole. Although this is the strongest punishment possible in a UK court, many have raised the question of whether this is actually justice.

Those opposing the arguments of bringing back the death penalty have suggested that it is not humane to condemn someone for killing and then perform the same action themselves. Some supporters of Rasul have even suggested that he didn't mean to kill the Lewis family and therefore his punishment shouldn't be so severe.

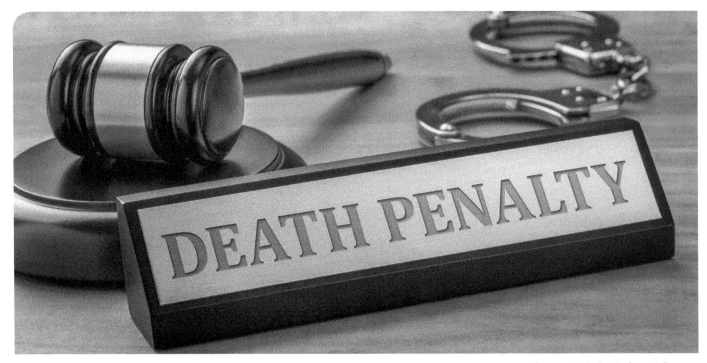

Figure 3.19 Capital punishment

Activities ?

1   What crime has Rasul been convicted of committing?

2   Why is there a debate concerning his case?

3   Use information from the article and from the rest of this chapter to write down arguments for and against capital punishment. Discuss these with a partner. Which arguments do you feel are stronger? Why?

4   Do you think Rasul's Islamic faith should be part of the discussion concerning his punishment? Why or why not?

5   Write a response to the newspaper article giving your opinion on the matter. What arguments would you use to support your viewpoint?

6   Why does this article show how controversial the issue of crime and punishment can be?

7   In groups, debate the following statements:

   a   'If more was done to tackle the causes of crime, there would be less crime.'

   b   'Islam has the right idea in supporting capital punishment.'

   c   'Justice for the victim is the only consideration in cases where a crime has been committed.'

Vote at the end of each debate to decide which arguments you think are strongest and give your reasons why.

Exam tips

- Always demonstrate factual knowledge in every question you answer. Use Islamic terms when appropriate and make sure you explain them fully.

- When being asked to give your own opinion, make sure you support each point you make with reasoned evidence. Try to be as persuasive as possible in your responses.

- Always read questions carefully before answering them to give yourself thinking time to check you fully understand the question.

Can you remember?

- Why are beliefs and actions so important to Muslims?
- Why is Islam viewed as a religion of peace?
- Why are ideas of justice so important to Muslims and how are these seen within sources of authority in Islam?
- What are the Five Pillars of Islam and how do they relate to issues surrounding crime and punishment?
- What does jihad mean and how important is this to Muslims in their daily lives?
- Why do Muslims believe it is important to support and help others, even those who are criminals who have committed crimes in society?

4 Peace and conflict

Conflict is an ever-growing issue in today's world. Threats from terrorism, as well as disputes within and between countries and nations, mean that war, the threat of war and all the challenges that come with it are more common today than ever before. Often, religion is seen by many to be at the heart of conflict between nations.

Islam, as with all other world religions, offers teachings on war, conflict and peace. Muslims in the world today hope and work for peace for themselves and for others. However, despite this, most would also agree that peace is a hard idea to put into practice or fully achieve. The big religious question is why peace is so hard to achieve if so many want it for the world?

One understanding of the word 'Islam' is that it means 'peace'. Muslims believe Islam is a peaceful religion. Another understanding of 'Islam' is 'submission to Allah', which suggests ideas of peace in a Muslim giving themselves to do what they believe Allah wants. The Islamic understanding of peace can be understood best through exploration of ideas such as justice and equality. This is because Muslims accept that peace within the world can only be achieved once the world is a just and fair place for everyone.

The Qur'an is full of teachings that support ideas of peace, and practices which advocate helping others and living in peaceful harmony with others. There are many examples of Islamic organisations working to try to achieve peace and unity within the religion of Islam and between Muslims and other religious groups.

In today's world it is easy to name examples of conflict, including those which are directly related to religion. Due to media attention, many people today mistakenly associate Islam with ideas of terrorism and view the religion and all its followers as enemies. It is clear that there is a minority of people who claim to be Muslim and perform atrocities in the name of Allah but this is not the 'true' nature of the religion of Islam, which Muslims wish to promote.

Learning objectives

In this chapter you will find out about:

- Muslim attitudes towards peace
- the role of Muslims in peacemaking
- Muslim attitudes to conflict
- pacifism
- Just War theory
- Holy War
- weapons of mass destruction
- issues surrounding conflict

Checkpoint

Recall

Before starting this chapter, you should remember:

- Islam is a religion of peace
- Muslims believe in one God called Allah
- Muslims understand Islam to be a religion where they submit to Allah in everything they do
- Islam is a religion that has followers in every country in the world
- Muslims believe and teach that ideas such as justice, forgiveness, reconciliation and peace are important
- there are two main branches in Islam. Sunni and Shi'a Muslims interpret and practice their faith in slightly different ways
- Muslims refer to sources of authority such as their holy book, the Qur'an, when considering what the right action should be in any given situation.

4.1 Muslim attitudes towards peace

Learning objectives

- To understand the nature and importance of peace for Muslims.
- To explore Muslim teachings about peace.
- To consider why Islam is a religion of peace.

Figure 4.1 Muslims gather at a peace demonstration in March 2003 in Jakarta, Indonesia

The nature of peace

Peace is something all people in society strive for. It is generally accepted and understood as an absence of war or conflict. However, the idea of peace is seen to have a wider interpretation within the religion of Islam. For Muslims, peace is not just about an absence of war. Muslims are not pacifists and Islam does teach that war may be necessary in certain circumstances in order to bring about the desired goal of peace. For Muslims, peace is the absence of oppression, corruption, injustice and tyranny. In other words, Islam understands peace to be directly related to justice and the idea of a world where fairness is the guiding principle.

Why is peace important for Muslims?

Events such as the suicide attacks of 11 September 2001 in New York, and other terrorist acts such as the Paris attacks of November 2015, have been attributed to a small number of people who claim to be Muslim and say they are performing atrocities in the name of Allah. Following such events there has been a need to challenge stereotypes associated with Islam and show those outside the faith what the true meaning of being a Muslim and following the faith of Islam is about. As a result of media coverage, many people distrust Muslims and only associate the religion with terrorism. Islam is a religion of peace and its followers are keen to illustrate that it is not a religion of conflict.

What does Islam teach about peace?

Islam is a religion that is intended for a peaceful society. Muslims believe that Allah created the world with the intention that his people would live by the moral code he set, which would instil ideas of love, compassion, peace and love. The Qur'an teaches that Muslims should strive for peace and that even when they may face criticism and hate from others who may not understand their faith, they should respond with words of peace.

Muslims believe that the idea of peace is related to the idea of jihad in Islam. This is a term often misunderstood by those outside of Islam who think it is only associated with holy war. Muslims understand jihad in two ways. The first is to do with holy war, or lesser jihad, which is justified according to a set criteria. The second and more important understanding of jihad is a personal struggle for peace, or greater jihad, for each Muslim through resisting temptations in life and trying to live peaceful lives, following the rules given to them by Allah.

The ummah is of utmost importance in Islam. This is the worldwide community of Muslims to which every follower of Islam belongs. Muslims believe they should try to live in peace with each other and work to support each other.

However, Islam does teach that sometimes war may be necessary in order to bring about peace. Muslims accept that although war is never wanted, it is recognised that it may have a purpose in the fight to achieve peace. This is stated in the Qur'an.

Muslims believe that through standing up against injustice in the world and trying to help everyone be equal, they will be contributing towards a just society. Islam teaches that it is through this that peace can be achieved in the world.

Islam as a religion of peace

In recent times, media reports and the actions of a minority have resulted in Islam being associated with conflict and terrorist acts. However, the true understanding of Islam is that it is a religion of peace. Since the suicide attacks of 11 September 2001 in New York, politicians have been criticised for making such associations and have therefore made efforts to distinguish between those claiming to be Muslims but performing terrorist acts and Islam itself as a religion. The majority of Muslims would want to show to others that they are not violent and do not support the use of violence. They recognise that peace is important and it is only through co-operation, respect and shared understanding that this can be achieved. Muslims believe it is important to be at peace with others in their daily lives. They recognise that they may not always get on with everyone, but they should work to overcome conflict they may face. Muslims believe that when they argue with others, they should be the first to try to reconcile with them. They also believe that they should forgive others when they do wrong and apologise rather than hold grudges. Muslims believe that the key teachings of Islam as a religion of peace should be applied in all aspects of the life of individual Muslims, as Allah intended.

Sources of authority

O you who believe! Enter into Islam wholeheartedly; and follow not the footsteps of the Evil One; for he is to you an avowed enemy.
(Surah, 2:208)

And the servants of (Allah) Most Gracious are those who walk on the earth in humility, and when the ignorant address them, they say, 'Peace!' (Surah, 25:63)

Sources of authority

To those against whom war is made, permission is given (to fight), because they are wronged – and verily, Allah is Most Powerful for their aid. (Surah 22:39)

But if the enemy incline towards peace, do you (also) incline towards peace, and trust in Allah: for He is the One that hears and knows (all things). (Surah 8:61)

Activities ?

1   Do you think peace is important in the world today? What arguments can you come up with to support this idea? Write your thoughts down.

2   Write a response to the following question making sure you explain ideas fully. What does the religion of Islam teach about peace?

3   Imagine you have been asked to write a letter to someone who has misconceptions about Islam. They believe Islam is a religion that supports conflict. What would you write to show them why their view may be wrong?

4   'If religion were removed, there would be peace in the world.' Consider this statement. In pairs, create a list of arguments that agree with the statement and arguments that disagree with it. Mark the ones that you think are strongest and explain why.

Exam-style question

Outline three Muslims beliefs about peace. **(3 marks)**

Extend your knowledge

Muslims believe that inner peace is also important in Islam. The Five Pillars of Islam, which are the basic duties that every Muslim should perform, are accepted as helping to develop the idea of inner peace. The actions of the Shahadah, Salah, Zakah, Sawm and Hajj help Muslims to understand how they should behave within their lives. Muslims believe they develop self-discipline through performing these actions, which helps to develop inner peace. They also demonstrate ideas of justice and equality which Muslims believe will help to achieve peace in the world.

Exam tip

This question asks for three beliefs that would be held by a Muslim about the idea of peace. Make sure you write three separate sentences with a different belief in each one to achieve the three marks available.

Summary

- Muslims widen their understanding of the term 'peace' to include the absence of injustice and unfairness.
- Islam is considered to be a religion of peace.
- Some people may fear Islam and believe it is not a religion of peace because they think it is associated with terrorism.
- The Qur'an contains many teachings about peace.
- Islam does accept that sometimes war is necessary in order to bring about peace in the world.
- Peace can be related to ideas such as jihad and is seen within the Five Pillars of Islam.

Checkpoint

Strengthen

S1 What is the Islamic understanding of 'peace'?

S2 What does the Qur'an teach about peace?

S3 How is Islam seen as a religion of peace?

Challenge

C1 Do you think it is a fair assumption for people not to understand that Islam is a religion of peace?

C2 Why do you think Muslims are so concerned with ensuring their religion is accurately represented?

C3 Do you think Muslims can do more as a religion to ensure Islam is accurately represented?

4.2 Muslims and peacemaking

Learning objectives

- To understand Muslim teachings about peacemaking.
- To explore the importance of justice, forgiveness and reconciliation in peacemaking.
- To understand the work of Muslims working for peace today.

Islam and peacemaking

Muslims believe peace is important and try to work towards achieving this. Muslims work for justice, equality between people and a fair society in the world. Protecting human rights, peace and freedom are essential principles in Islam. Furthermore, Muslims believe working for peace in the world is a responsibility. This is a teaching seen within duties such as khalifah where Muslims believe they should act as stewards, caring for the world and everything within it as it was created by Allah.

Justice, forgiveness and reconciliation

Justice, forgiveness and reconciliation are instrumental for Muslims in understanding and achieving peace. They believe that they have been commanded to work for justice by Allah and that this is an instruction given to them through the teaching of the Prophet Muhammad and in the Qur'an. Muslims are taught to work for justice and stand up when they are faced with examples of injustice. Islam also teaches that it is important to forgive those who do wrong and try, if possible, to reconcile with them.

Muslims believe that justice, forgiveness and reconciliation are important in peacemaking because:

- they believe that all humans were created by Allah to be equal, whatever their race, culture or gender
- Muslims believe that Allah is just. It is believed that he will treat everyone with justice and fairness, and Muslims believe they too should act this way in the world. By doing this, it will help people to live together peacefully. The Qur'an teaches the importance of justice and that Allah intended there to be justice within society
- Muslims believe conflict should be resolved using forgiveness and reconciliation as Islam teaches that Allah is merciful. The name of Allah 'the merciful'

(Ar Rahim) is repeated many times during prayer. Muslims believe they should follow his example to try to bring about peace

- the Qur'an contains teachings relating to ideas of forgiveness and reconciliation, such as Surah 41:31–38
- there are some actions in Islam that display ideas of forgiveness and equality. Muslims stand on Mount Arafat during Hajj to ask for forgiveness from Allah. They attend Hajj as equals, performing the same actions, wearing the same clothes and completing this Pillar in the same way to show they are all equal before Allah. Hajj is an example of how Muslims are at peace with each other.

Muslims can sometimes be seen to promote ideas associated with the ethical theory of **situation ethics**. In cases where a person has done something wrong due to their situation, or circumstance, it often produces feelings of sorrow. Muslims advocate trying to help people in this situation, perhaps by offering solutions to improve their lives rather than to punish them severely as their actions may require.

Sources of authority

Nor can Goodness and Evil be equal. Repel (Evil) with what is better: then will he between whom and you was hatred become as it were your friend and intimate! And no one will be granted such goodness except those who exercise patience and self-restraint,—none but persons of the greatest good fortune. And if (at any time) an incitement to discord is made to you by the Evil One, seek refuge in Allah. He is the One Who hears and knows all things. (Surah 41:34–36)

Allah commands justice, the doing of good, and liberality to all kith and kin … (Surah 16:90)

We sent aforetime Our messengers with Clear Signs and sent down with them the Book and the Balance (of Right and Wrong), that men may stand forth in justice… (Surah 57:25)

Sources of authority

The recompense for an injury is an injury equal thereto (in degree): but if a person forgives and makes reconciliation, his reward is due from Allah… (Surah 42:40)

Figure 4.2 Islamic Relief, a charity founded in 1948

Sources of authority

… and if anyone saved a life, it would be as if he saved the life of the whole people… (Surah 5:32)

Figure 4.3 Salaam Peace uses sports, media and education initiatives to bring people together

How do Muslims work for peace today?

Muslims work for peace in many different ways. They believe that by following the duties such as the Five Pillars of Islam, they are working for justice. Muslims are encouraged to fast during the month of Ramadan for the pillar of Sawm. This is to better understand the plight of the poor and needy. Similarly, Zakah is where Muslims are expected to give 2.5 per cent of their residual wealth to help the poor and needy. They can also choose to give sadaqah, which is voluntary charity, at any time. Many Muslims also support campaigns and organisations that work for peace in the world.

Islamic Relief

Islamic Relief was founded initially to help the victims of war. It has worked in countries such as Bosnia, Somalia and Iraq. Today, the organisation responds when disasters and emergencies occur but it has a wider role in trying to help communities to live sustainable lives and address the causes of poverty. Its members feel that through striving to make a difference to people's lives, they can work to achieve peace within the world. They believe that the Qur'an commands them to help others.

Islamic Relief works for peace through:

- raising awareness of the challenges faced by children who live in extreme poverty, hardship or countries of conflict, and raising money to help them
- providing teachers and materials for children most hit by poverty, so they have the opportunity to learn and make the most of their lives
- supporting refugees with medical care and food in countries such as Syria where people have been forced to flee their homes to escape war and conflict
- providing emergency aid and relief when a disaster happens.

Salaam Peace

Salaam Peace is a community engagement programme in Waltham Forest and Hackney in London. This area of London has one of the most diverse populations in the UK and the organisation was established in an attempt to change the perception of Muslims in Britain, following the suicide attacks in New York on 11 September 2001 and in London on 7 July 2005. It aims to bring people together in the community and work for peace and harmony through:

- sports activities including football and cycling, basketball, hockey and cricket initiatives
- homework clubs to provide support, help and guidance to children in the local community
- volunteering programmes and mentoring schemes to ensure every person in the community feels valued and to offer role models to raise achievement and celebrate success
- providing community activities to develop respect and understanding between groups from different backgrounds and religions.

Activities

1   Complete this sentence, making sure you explain each idea fully: 'I think peace is important/is not important in today's world because...'

2   'Achieving peace in the world is every person's responsibility.' Discuss this statement with a partner. Create a list of reasons why a person may agree with it and why a person may disagree with it.

3   Look at the Islamic organisations in this Topic that work for peace. Make a list of pros and cons of each activity, thinking about why one may be more successful and have more impact in achieving peace than another. Present your thoughts to the class.

Exam-style questions

Outline three ways in which Muslims try to work for peace today. **(3 marks)**

Exam tip

Make sure you explain three different ways clearly. Use the information about what organisations do to work for peace. Make sure you are specific in your response for each example.

Summary

- Muslims understand that justice, forgiveness and reconciliation are closely related to ideas of peace.
- The Qur'an teaches Muslims that they have a duty to work for justice and reconciliation in the world and through doing this peace can be achieved.
- Muslims perform the Five Pillars of Islam, which can be seen to promote ideas of peace and justice.

Checkpoint

Strengthen

S1 What does Islam teach about the importance of peace and peacemaking?

S2 How do Islamic organisations work for peace today?

S3 How do the quotes in the Sources of authority feature boxes show the importance of the Six Beliefs of Islam?

Challenge

C1 How successful do you think the work of Islamic organisations are in working for peace?

C2 Do you think opinions of Islam have changed since Islamic organisations started raising awareness of community cohesion?

C3 How important do you think it is for Muslims to work for peace in the world today?

4.3 Muslim attitudes to conflict

Learning outcomes

- To understand the nature and causes of conflict.
- To identify the problems conflict leads to within society.
- To explore Muslim responses to the causes of conflict.

The nature of conflict

Conflict is a clash, or a serious disagreement or argument. This can be on a small scale, where one person falls out with another. For example, bullying can be seen as a form of conflict, where one person picks on another for some reason. On a larger scale, nations of people are in conflict with each other, for example, the war in Syria. Conflict within the world today is often blamed on religion, although there may also be other contributing factors. It is fair to say that conflict mostly arises for a combination of reasons. The impact of conflict is that it can lead to serious tension between groups of people, which could be expressed through acts of terrorism or war. This, in turn, has a wider impact, affecting other countries and people, too.

Sources of authority

If two parties among the Believers fall into a quarrel, make you peace between them: but if one of them transgresses beyond bounds against the other, then fight you (all) against the one that transgresses until it complies with the command of Allah; but if it complies, then make peace between them with justice, and be fair: for Allah loves those who are fair (and just).
(Surah 49:9)

Causes of conflict

There are usually a number of causes for any conflict.

Politics

Politics concerns beliefs about ruling and organising a country. When there is a lack of unity this can be a major cause of conflict, as strong feelings about different views can lead to tension between people and a breakdown in communication. It may be that one group believes they have a stronger right to hold political power, or they believe that a country's rulers are not acting in the best interests of the people and should be challenged. An example of this could be seen in the conflict in Syria, where a lack of unity has led to challenges for political power.

Resources

Conflict can often arise as a result of demand and greed for resources. This could include economical resources, such as money, or natural resources, such as oil or gas, that a country may have. Resources could also involve the desire for land and power. If another country or group of people believes they have a right to these resources and tries to take them by force, this could lead to war. An example of this can be seen in the 19th century, when European countries began building empires in Africa and Asia to gain power and resources, which led to conflict between them.

History

History is an important factor in people or countries being in conflict with each other. Often the history of land or a people is not easily forgotten and is remembered each time there is the threat of further conflict. There may be long-standing disputes over who has rights to land as well as possible ethnic and religious differences. These can lead to conflicts never really being resolved, as one group may feel they have been treated unfairly and not given what they are entitled to. An example of this contributing to conflict can be seen in the breakup of Yugoslavia in the 1990s.

Culture

Culture is the ideas, customs and way of life of a group of people or society. The differences that exist between different cultures can be a cause of conflict between people. Often there may be bad feeling between groups of people, especially if one group feels they have more rights than others. This could lead to acts of discrimination where groups of people, particularly minorities, are treated differently in a society. An example of this has been seen in the Second World War, with the way the Jews and other minority groups were treated under the rule of Hitler and the Nazis in Germany.

Religion

Religion is often a reason given for the occurrence of conflict. Differences in faith with one group of people believing their faith is the only true faith may cause division and disunity. Some religious believers may hold certain views because of their religion and argue that they are entitled to land or resources because of the history of their religion. Religion can also lead to division in society where there is a challenge from those who are not religious. The world today is **pluralistic**, which means there are many religions, spiritualities and faiths. This can lead to tensions existing between people. Examples of this could be seen in the challenge between the Jews and the Muslims in Israel and Palestine.

Can you remember?

- Why is justice important for Muslims?
- What are the Five Roots of 'Usul ad-Din?
- Why do Muslims believe humans suffer?

Why does conflict cause problems within society?

Conflict causes problems in society because:

- most conflicts involve different groups of people who feel they have nothing in common with each other and no shared beliefs
- it can have a negative effect on community relations, with groups not willing to integrate. This can lead to some minority groups feeling left out and isolated within their community. This can be seen where groups of religious believers build their own communities, causing an unnecessary divide between them and others
- it can lead to disunity and distrust where groups of people with different beliefs or backgrounds cannot get along in society. This can be seen in situations where there is discrimination and different groups treat each other badly
- there is often very little agreement or compromise so it is very difficult to get people to talk, work together or live in peace without conflicts arising. In some communities, people from different groups will not mix or integrate
- it can lead to poor treatment, discrimination and even physical violence by one group to another. This can then in turn lead to reprisals.

How do Muslims respond to the causes of conflict?

Muslims believe that they should work for peace as this is what Allah intended. This means working to try to live in harmony in communities and with people from other

backgrounds and religions. Islam teaches that Muslims should try to help others and work for justice in the world and this will help to bring peace.

However, despite its emphasis on peacemaking, Islam also teaches that there may be occasions when conflict is justified. In the history of Islam, there have been instances where Muslims have needed to defend themselves and the religion of Islam, which is taught as acceptable. In its early history there are many examples of Muslims losing their lives trying to defend their beliefs and values, including the followers of Muhammad at the Battle of Mu'tah in 629 CE. Islam does recognise that there will always be differences, and therefore conflict between people, and sets out rules for conflict to take place. This appears contradictory, with Islam providing advice and guidelines to minimise conflict yet also offering rules for war. However, Muslims point out that violence is never advocated by Islam to simply attack someone. If violence is necessary, the only justification is that it is in a situation where a Muslim needs to defend Islam. Outside of this, a Muslim would be in the wrong if they initiated conflict with another. This could be seen to be in line with the ethical theory of situation ethics, where each situation needs to be considered individually in order to decide on the best action to take.

The Qur'an Surah 2:190–195 teaches Muslims that they should fight if the need arises, if it is done for Allah and is appropriate to the situation. Muslims do not believe that Islam teaches that they should always fight, but only when it is the right action to take. For example, if Muslims themselves or the religion of Islam was being attacked, they should defend it. This seems to agree with situation ethics in that sometimes conflict is needed in order to bring peace.

Sources of authority

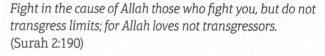

Fight in the cause of Allah those who fight you, but do not transgress limits; for Allah loves not transgressors.
(Surah 2:190)

Non-religious attitudes and Humanist views

Humanists and other **atheists** promote ideas of peace and harmony. Atheists do not follow any religion or hold belief in any god but may hold similar views to Muslims, such as the importance of ending conflict to bring about peace and harmony. Humanists seek to live good lives without harming others. They believe it is important to use reason and experience when making decisions. This means they would not want conflict in the world and would work to promote peace by finding solutions that reduce conflict and its causes. Many non-religious followers may actually believe that religion is at the root of many conflicts, as differences between people due to their beliefs or diversity within religious views have led to many wars over time. Although this belief could be accepted as true in some cases, Muslims would still argue that conflict is not desired, although it is sometimes needed in order to bring about peace.

Sources of authority

And hold fast, all together, by the Rope which Allah (stretches out for you), and be not divided among yourselves; and remember with gratitude Allah's favour on you; for you were enemies and He joined your hearts in love, so that by His Grace you became brethren; and you were on the brink of the Pit of Fire, and He saved you from it. Thus does Allah make His Signs clear to you: that you may be guided. (Surah 3:103)

Exam-style question

Explain two ways Muslims respond to conflict.
(4 marks)

Activities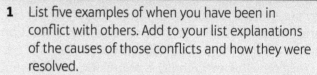

1. List five examples of when you have been in conflict with others. Add to your list explanations of the causes of those conflicts and how they were resolved.

2. Do you think conflict is caused by one factor alone or is it often a combination of factors? Give reasons for your answer, referring to specific examples of conflict if possible. Try to find examples that have not been mentioned in this topic.

3. In pairs, consider arguments for and against the following statement: 'If we were to remove religion, we would not have conflict in the world.' Share your arguments with another pair before having a class debate on this topic.

Exam tip

This question is asking you to offer two different ways that Muslims may respond to conflict. You will be awarded one mark for stating each reason and a second mark for developing it fully.

Summary

- Conflict occurs when there is a serious argument or disagreement.
- There are many causes of conflict including: politics, resources, history, culture and religion.
- Many people feel religion is often the main cause of conflict or war between groups of people.
- Conflict can cause problems within society including tension, disunity, discrimination, a lack of trust and a lack of compromise. The Qur'an offers guidance on how Muslims should work for peace, but also rules for when it may be acceptable to go to war or fight.
- Muslims believe conflict is justified if they are defending Islam.

Checkpoint

Strengthen

S1 What are the causes of conflict?
S2 What problems can conflict cause in society?
S3 How do Muslims respond to conflict?

Challenge

C1 What do you think is the biggest problem conflict causes in society and why?
C2 Do you think it is possible for conflict to be overcome in communities?
C3 Why do you think Muslims believe they are right to defend Islam if it is attacked?

4.4 Pacifism

Learning outcomes:

- To understand the nature and history of pacifism.
- To explore Muslim teachings about passive resistance.
- To identify ways that passive resistance is used by Muslims.

What is pacifism?

Figure 4.5 The symbol for peace

Pacifism is the belief that war and violence are unjustifiable, and that conflict should be settled by peaceful means. The term 'pacifism' was first used by the French peace campaigner Emile Arnaud and was adopted by other peace activists at the tenth annual Universal Peace Congress in 1901. The practice of pacifism can be traced back in history. Pacifists refuse to be involved in any form of war or conflict. Many of the 16,000 British men who refused to fight in the First World War did this because of their belief in pacifism. Some did take part in the war as stretcher bearers and ambulance drivers. Within religion, pacifism has been widely associated with Jesus in Christianity, with many believing he was a pacifist advocating ideas of non-violence, as well as the Quakers, a Christian movement who are well known for their pacifist views and teachings. Pacifism has also been associated with eastern religions such as the idea of **ahimsa** non-violence within Hinduism.

Islam and pacifism

Many religions advocate and support ideas of pacifism. Islam, however, is not a pacifist religion. Islam does support ideas of peace and peacemaking but accepts that war may be required in certain situations when all other methods have been tried and have failed. Some

Muslims beleive that Surah 5:27–30 supports ideas of pacifism. They accept that it could be interpreted to mean that if a person does something to another person, it is not right to retaliate with violence. In particular, it could be argued that Surah 5:28 supports ideas of pacifism. Others, however, argue that the true interpretation of this verse is not that one person should surrender to another, but that a person should not initiate aggression towards another. Therefore, if something happens to a person as the result of another, some Muslims may interpret this to mean that they are justified in responding, but it should be without violence. This is one of many examples of the diversity that exists within Islamic beliefs surrounding ideas such as pacifism.

Sources of authority

If you do stretch your hand against me, to slay me, it is not for me to stretch my hand against you to slay you: for I do fear Allah, the Cherisher of the worlds.
(Surah 5:28)

There are examples within the history of Islam where Muhammad was forced to use violence in order to deal with challenges he faced in his life. One occurred after Muhammad began to receive the revelations of the Qur'an from Allah through the angel Jibril. He began to pass the messages on slowly and while some chose to follow him, others used violence and threatened him and his followers. This led to Muhammad being forced to leave Makkah, an event known as the **Hijrah**.

Some have argued that initially Muhammad adopted more pacifist tendencies and tried to ignore the violence used against him, but eventually he had to use violence to respond. Today, violence is not rejected completely by Islam but ideas of peace are promoted more strongly.

Some scholars have identified pacifist traits in examples within Islam, although there is general agreement that Islam is not a pacifist religion. Some have argued that

Sufism, a mystical branch of Islam, is a tradition that can be seen as a pacifist movement. It has in the past tended to emphasise the love of fellow men as an extension of the teaching of the love of Allah. Sufis stress the importance of an internal struggle but even so, the majority recognise the need for the use of violence in defence of Islam after all other methods of reconciliation have been tried.

What does Islam teach about passive resistance?

Passive resistance is the belief in non-violent protest or resistance to authority. The objector makes a choice not to respond to conflict in a violent way. It must be understood, however, that passive resistance does not mean a lack of action. The objector shows their disagreement with the authority or law by non-violent means, for example, sit-ins, boycotts or peaceful protests. The Ahmadiyya Muslim Community are a group founded in 1889 and seen today in many countries all over the world. They have organised rallies and non-violent protests to highlight issues of concern as shown in **Figure 4.6**. Here they are protesting about how terms such as 'jihad' are misunderstood by non-Muslims as well as Muslims, some of whom are being drawn into the misconception, mistakenly believing they are choosing to fight for the right reasons.

- Islam teaches that Muslims should always work for peace and that Muslims should not be the first to attack.
- 'Islam' is understood by Muslims to mean 'submission to Allah' and this means they must work for peace in co-operative and peaceful ways. They believe their aim should be to co-exist peacefully with all other people.
- Islam advocates passive resistance (non-violent protest) so, if displeased with something in society or an action of the law, Muslims could choose to protest peacefully by marching, writing letters to politicians to bring about change or signing petitions.
- Some Muslims have tried to educate others about protesting peacefully. Nafez Assaily is a Sufi Muslim who grew up in Hebron in Palestine. He emphasises the need for dialogue, education and service to the poor in order to promote ideas of non-violence. He set up a mobile book loan service called the 'Library on Wheels for Non-violence and Peace' to try and promote ideas of peace and non-violence.

Arab Spring

'Arab Spring' refers to democratic uprisings that happened independently across the Arab world in 2011. The movement is believed to have originated in Tunisia in December 2010 and quickly spread to countries such as Egypt, Syria, Libya, Saudi Arabia, Yemen and Jordan. Although many of the uprisings used violence, some of them chose not to use violence to voice their dissatisfaction with local governments and their use of power. Some protesters tried to use the political system to remove oppressors, while others chose to protest peacefully through demonstrations or social media. Some involved in the movement were nominated for the Nobel Peace Prize.

Figure 4.6 Peaceful protest by the Ahmadiyya Muslim Community

Sources of authority

But Allah does call to the Home of Peace: He does guide whom He pleases to a way that is straight. To those who do right is a goodly (reward)—Indeed, more (than in measure)! No darkness nor shame shall cover their faces! They are companions of the Garden; they will abide therein (for ever)!
(Surah 10:25–26)

Activities ?

1   What reasons do you think a person might give to explain why they are a pacifist?

2   Create a table to consider the advantages and disadvantages of the ideas of: violence, pacifism and passive resistance. After completing your table, write a paragraph explaining which of the three methods you would support and why.

3   Work in groups to think of something in the world you are not happy about, such as poverty, lack of clean water, the right to go to school, etc. Make a list of what actions you could use to show your disagreement with the situation and whether you agree with pacifist or passive resistance teachings. As a group, discuss which actions you think would be most effective and why. Present them to your class to see whether they agree with you.

Exam-style question

Explain two Muslim teachings about passive resistance. **(4 marks)**

Exam tip

You are required to explain two different teachings. Make sure you fully develop the first one by adding an explanation and an example, before moving on to present the second one in the same way.

Can you remember?

• Why is Muhammad important to Muslims?
• Why do Muslims believe they have to submit to Allah in everything they do?
• What does Islam teach about the conditions under which it is acceptable to fight for Allah?

Summary

• Pacifism is the term used to describe a person who opposes all forms of war and violence and will choose not to fight.
• Islam is not a pacifist religion. It recognises that there may be a need on some occasions to use violence in order to bring about peace.
• Passive resistance is when someone uses non-violent methods to show their disagreement with authority.
• Islam supports the use of passive resistance.
• Methods of passive resistance used by Muslims could include writing letters to bring an issue to the attention of members of the government, signing petitions or taking part in a protest march.

Checkpoint

Strengthen

S1 What is pacifism?

S2 Why is Islam not considered to be a pacifist religion?

S3 What is passive resistance and why would Muslims support its use?

Challenge

C1 Why is it a contradiction to say Islam is a religion of peace and yet it is not a pacifist religion?

C2 Why do you think some Muslims might oppose all forms of violence?

C3 How important do you feel passive resistance is to Islam?

4.5 Just War theory

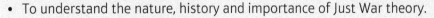

Learning outcomes:

- To understand the nature, history and importance of Just War theory.
- To consider the conditions of a just war and whether a just war is ever possible.
- To explore Muslim teachings on just war.

Nature and history of Just War theory

Just War theory is a doctrine or tradition that is found largely in Christian philosophy.

It is a combination of three elements:

- the idea that it is wrong to take human life
- yet countries need to protect their citizens and sometimes conflict or war may be needed in order to do this
- protecting innocent lives or important moral values sometimes requires the use of force.

It attempts to offer a set of accepted conditions for judging whether or not it is right to go to war. It also provides a concrete set of rules on how a just war should be fought. Although it originated with Christianity, believers of other religions and non-believers can use it as a suitable way to evaluate whether a war is just or not. The concept of Just War theory, however, is subjective. This means that individual Muslims, both Sunni and Shi'a, will interpret it differently according to their own view of the situation. This can make the theory difficult to apply in practice and means that the principles could be open to interpretation.

In Islam, Just War theory relates to the concept of jihad. Jihad literally means 'striving' and is generally understood to encompass two types. The first is greater jihad, which involves the inner personal struggle every Muslim experiences to resist temptation in their lives and follow the rules of Allah. The second, lesser jihad, relates to Just War theory as it is a set of rules that must be met in order for a war to be considered justified. However, it should be noted that Just War theory is emphasised differently by followers of Sunni and Shi'a Islam. Sunni Muslims do not give it any official status although it is recognised as a central idea. In comparison, Shi'a Muslims, especially in the Twelver sect, Jihad is recognised as one of the 10 central practices of the faith.

The word 'jihad' is often misused and misunderstood, both by Muslims and people outside of the religion. The media has at times, portrayed Islam as a warlike religion, having associated terrorist acts with jihad. Those who performed these acts also claim to be Muslim and have claimed it is jihad. In actual fact, Islam teaches that violence is wrong unless it is absolutely necessary to use it as a last resort in defence of the religion. It is wise to read Qur'anic passages, such as Surah 4:69–110, in order to understand the breadth of guidance supplied to Muslims prior to making negative associations with the term 'jihad'.

Sources of authority

To those against whom war is made, permission is given (to fight), because they are wronged – and verily, Allah is Most Powerful for their aid. (Surah 22:39)

Why is Just War theory important?

It is important because:

- it aims to provide a guide to the right way to act when there is the risk of conflict. It provides a set of rules that should be followed and met in this situation
- it provides a framework that can be used by individuals and political groups to assess whether the path of conflict or war is the best option to take
- it is not intended to justify wars but instead to prevent them. It helps to show that going to war, unless in exceptional circumstances, is wrong. It hopes to encourage those in dispute to find better, more peaceful methods of resolving the conflict.

What are the conditions for a just war for Muslims?

Islam teaches that a war will be just provided that it:

1 is declared by a religious leader not a political leader

2 has the support of the Muslim community and not be declared by one individual

3 is an act of defence not attack

4   does not aim to win new land or power

5   is not done to convert others to the religion of Islam

6   is a last resort and all peaceful methods of solving the conflict have already been tried

7   will not threaten or endanger innocent civilians, particularly women and children

8   will not harm trees, crops and animals.

Muslims accept the idea of jihad – understood to be a 'striving' for Allah. This is separated into greater jihad, a personal struggle to resist temptation in the daily life of a Muslim while living as Allah intended, and lesser jihad, which is holy war. There are references to this in the Qur'an, for example in Surah 4: 69–110, which appears to support the idea of fighting to protect Islam and provides criteria such as that offered in Just War theory.

Muslims believe that under these conditions they should fight because:

- the Qur'an teaches that Muslims can fight in self-defence
- Muhammad himself fought in some wars
- many of the Hadith statements seem to suggest war is allowed. The Qur'an teaches that anyone who dies in a just war will live on eternally in paradise, Al-Jannah.

> ### Sources of authority
>
> *Let those fight in the cause of Allah who sell the life of this world for the Hereafter. To him who fights in the cause of Allah – whether he is slain or gets victory – soon shall We give him a reward of great (value).* (Surah 4:74)

meet the criteria set. Being involved in conflict without threatening human life or damaging the environment would be difficult. The outcomes of war often mean gains for one side in terms of land, resources and power so it would also be difficult to assess this prior to the conflict taking place. However, ethical theories, such as situation ethics, can be applied in situations concerning Just War theory. By assessing each situation against the criteria individually, a logical and fair decision can be made for the benefit of the greater good.

Some people may also argue that modern weaponry cannot be used in a way that would satisfy the criteria of Just War theory. Weapons of mass destruction, for example, can cause widespread devastation. Furthermore, some Muslims argue that war, whether it fits the criteria or not, is never justified. Islam is a religion of peace and they may argue that non-violent methods can achieve peace. Some may even argue that violence only leads to more violence.

Is a just war ever actually possible?

Some people may think the religion of Islam offers contradictions when it comes to issues of war and peace. Islam promotes ideas of peace and peacemaking yet it has criteria for fighting in a war.

There can be seen to be diversity between Muslims on ascertaining whether a just war is actually possible. Some Muslims may argue that, as there is a set criteria of conditions which must be met, it is possible. Other Muslims might argue that a just war is never possible since it is challenging to

Figure 4.7 The innocent should be protected in war

Activities

1 Look at the conditions for a just war for Muslims. Are there any conditions that you would add to the list? Write down two suggestions with reasons for each one.

2 Do you think the criteria set for Just War theory in Islam is fair? Why or why not? Write a speech giving your opinion.

3 In groups, role play a discussion between a Muslim, a person from another religion and someone with no religious beliefs about Just War theory. Stay in role to ask each other questions about your views.

Extend your knowledge

The Siege of Jerusalem in 1187 ended when Balian of Ibelin agreed terms and surrendered the city to Saladin, the leader of the Islamic forces. Citizens who wished to leave were allowed to do so if they paid a ransom. Muslims slaves were also allowed to leave. This demonstrated Just War theory principles as everything possible was done to prevent bloodshed and fighting.

Exam-style question

Explain two reasons why Just War theory is important for Muslims. In your answer you must refer to a source of wisdom and authority. **(5 marks)**

Exam tip

You need to explain two different reasons, expanding on each one with detail or an example. Make sure you include reference to a source of authority and wisdom, such as the Qur'an.

Summary

- Just War theory primarily offers conditions to judge whether a war is the right action to take.
- Islam has its own interpretation of Just War theory and conditions for war.
- Muslims believe that Islam advocates peace but occasionally war may be justified if it meets these conditions in order to try to help achieve peace.
- Just War theory is important in providing guidelines for considering the option of war.
- Some people, including Muslims, believe that a just war is never possible.

Checkpoint

Strengthen

S1 What is Just War theory?

S2 What are the conditions in Islam for a just war?

S3 What does Islam teach about whether war is right or not?

Challenge

C1 Why might some people claim Just War theory is out of date in today's world?

C2 Why might the weapons used in warfare today not be compatible with Just War theory?

C3 How successful do you think Just War theory is when it is applied?

4.6 Holy war

Learning outcomes

- To understand the nature of holy war in Islam, known as **Harb al-Maqadis**.
- To explore Qur'anic teachings about war and peace.
- To consider Muslim teachings about war.

What is Harb al-Maqadis?

There are two ideas within Islam that relate to war. The first is jihad, which in itself is a term that can often be misunderstood. Jihad doesn't mean war but it is the struggle that Muslims believe is sometimes necessary in order to bring about peace. Muslims accept that they may need to sometimes fight and the conditions of lesser jihad offer them guidelines on when it is acceptable to do this. The second idea that is related to war in Islam is Harb al-Maqadis. This is usually understood as 'holy war', or a war that is fought because of religious differences. It is believed that Muhammad and his followers were involved in a number of holy wars including the Battle of Badr, the Battle of Uhud and the Conquest of Makkah.

Islam and Harb al-Maqadis

The Prophet Muhammad took part in many wars and it is believed that current Islamic teachings on war and peace stem from this.

For Muslims, holy war is only justifiable to defend the religion of Islam. This can then be further understood in a number of ways. In order for it to be a holy war, Muslims may fight to:

- protect the freedom of Muslims to practise their faith. If a country is preventing a Muslim from following the religion of Islam or even forcing them to practise a different faith, war would be considered justifiable in defence of Islam

- strengthen Islam. If the religion of Islam is being threatened in any way, this would be considered justifiable

- protect Muslims against an attack. If Muslims are being persecuted or are in danger of being attacked, Islam would consider it justifiable to fight.

There are also set conditions, taken from the teachings of the Qur'an which should be met for Muslims in a holy war. These hold many similarities with the conditions set for Just War theory.

The conditions for a holy war are that:

- the opponent must have started the fighting. Muslims can only act in self-defence and not start conflict
- it must not be fought to gain territory
- it must be launched by a religious leader

Figure 4.8 The Battle of Badr

Sources of authority

Fight in the cause of Allah those who fight you, but do not transgress limits; for Allah loves not transgressors. (Surah 2:190)

Sources of authority

But when the forbidden months are past, then fight and slay the Pagans wherever you find them, and seize them, beleaguer them, and lie in wait for them in every stratagem (of war); but if they repent, and establish regular prayers and practise regular charity, then open the way for them: for Allah is Oft-Forgiving, Most Merciful. (Surah 9:5)

Sources of authority

But if the enemy incline towards peace, do you (also) incline towards peace, and trust in Allah: for He is the One that hears and knows (all things). (Surah 8:61)

Sources of authority

Wherewith Allah guides all who seek His good pleasure to ways of peace and safety, and leads them out of darkness, by his Will, unto the light – guides them to a Path that is Straight. (Surah 5:16)

- it must be fought to bring about the end goal of good
- it must be a last resort. All other methods of solving the conflict peacefully should have been tried first
- innocent people should not be targeted or killed
- women should not be abused or raped
- enemies should still be treated with justice
- wounded enemy soldiers should be cared for and treated in the same way as one's own soldiers
- the war should stop as soon as the enemy asks for peace
- property should not be targeted or damaged
- chemical or biological warfare is forbidden.

There are, therefore, divergent Muslim views and teachings on war which lead to differences in opinions on whether it is right or wrong. Some may refer to teachings which advocate the acceptance of war when needed, while others may focus specifically on passages in the Qur'an that suggest war is never the answer to bring about peace.

What does the Qur'an say about war and peace?

The Qur'an is very clear that Muslims should only fight in defence of Islam.

Muslims believe that peace is important and war should only be a last resort. If peace can be attained, Muslims are instructed to accept it as this is the better option. Lesser jihad, which has been covered in the previous chapter, shows that war (holy war) should only be considered under certain circumstances and as a last resort. They also believe that Allah is forgiving and that this is important in achieving peace.

The Qur'an reinforces the idea of peace by making reference to the names of Allah, one being 'As salaam' which means 'peace'. Furthermore, the Qur'an emphasises that Islam is the path to peace. Surah 5:16 means that although Islam recognises war may sometimes be necessary, peace is the main idea which is promoted throughout the religion.

Muslims may hold divergent views about ideas of war and peace, which can also be seen within sources of authority such as the Qur'an. There appear to be some passages which support ideas of peace whilst others seem to advocate war. This can especially be seen within ideas of jihad which is a striving for Allah. Lesser jihad is often understood to mean 'holy war', suggesting that if a given set of criteria are met, it is right to fight. Passages in the Qur'an, however, such as Surah 8:61 and Surah 9:1–14 appear to advocate ideas of peace, recognising that although fighting is sometimes justified and required to bring about peace, so too are ideas of forgiveness and compassion.

Activities

1 Discuss the following questions in groups and feed back to your class:

   a Do you think the conditions set for Harb al-Maqadis are fair? Why or why not?

   b Do you think they are relevant for war today? Why or why not?

   c Is there anything you would add or change about them?

2 Summarise each quote from the Qur'an in your own words.

3 In groups, imagine you are hosting an interview between a Muslim and a pacifist about the topic of war. Create a set of questions that you would ask and consider how each of them would answer. Use your knowledge and the information in this topic to role play how it would go.

Exam-style questions

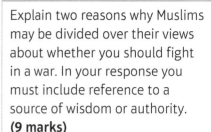

Explain two reasons why Muslims may be divided over their views about whether you should fight in a war. In your response you must include reference to a source of wisdom or authority. **(9 marks)**

Exam tip

War is a complex issue in Islam because there are different understandings of the idea of war (jihad and Harb al-Maqadis) and conditions set for when war would be justified. Your answers need to take this into account. Make sure you give two different reasons and use quotes from a source of wisdom or authority.

Can you remember?

- What do Muslims believe about lesser jihad?
- What do Muslims believe about how they should try to bring about peace?
- What does the Qur'an teach about peace?

Summary

- Harb al-Maqadis is an Islamic term and description for holy war.
- This is different to the Islamic ideas of lesser jihad.
- Muslims believe the Qur'an commands them to fight only in the defence of Islam.
- Islam teaches that defending Islam can include defending Muslims who are not allowed to practise their faith, strengthening Islam and protecting Muslims from attack.
- There are set conditions about Harb al-Maqadis that should be followed.

Checkpoint

Strengthen

S1 What is Harb al-Maqadis?

S2 What are the conditions for Harb al-Maqadis?

S3 What does the Qur'an say about war and peace for Muslims?

Challenge

C1 Why do you think the Qur'an gives war as a last resort?

C2 Do you think many wars fit the conditions of Harb al-Maqadis?

C3 Why might some people argue that the conditions of Harb al-Maqadis may not apply to wars that are fought in today's world?

4.7 Weapons of mass destruction

Learning objectives:

- To understand the problems and benefits of weapons of mass destruction.
- To explore Muslim attitudes towards the use of weapons of mass destruction.
- To understand atheist and Humanist attitudes towards the use of weapons of mass destruction.

Can you remember?

- What do Muslims believe about capital punishment?
- Why do Muslims believe humans suffer?
- What are the conditions in Islam for a just war?

Sources of authority

…that if anyone slew a person – unless it be for murder or for spreading mischief in the land – it would be as if he slew the whole people: and if anyone saved a life, it would be as if he saved the life of the whole people. … (Surah 5:32)

What are weapons of mass destruction?

Weapons of mass destruction (WMD) are nuclear, biological or chemical weapons that are able to cause death and destruction on a massive scale. Throughout history, weapons have developed as technology has advanced and more knowledge has been gained about how best to attack enemies. Perhaps the best known examples of the use of WMD are the nuclear bombings of Hiroshima and Nagasaki, in Japan, during the Second World War. It was difficult to assess the full extent of casualties, although it is believed that up to 135,000 people died in Hiroshima and 64,000 in Nagasaki, with roughly half the deaths occurring on the first day. During the following months, large numbers died from burns, radiation sickness and other illnesses connected to the atomic bombs, as well as poverty issues. Many of those who did survive were left with serious health problems as a result of the bombs.

What are the benefits and problems of WMD?

Today, war has changed significantly from the past. Countries realise there is a need to protect the vulnerable, such as civilians caught in a war zone, and to challenge injustices within the world. There is also a moral element, which should be considered when it comes to war. Theories such as Just War theory suggest conditions under which wars should be fought in order to minimise their impact. Some people claim there is no benefit to having WMD except to cause destruction and devastation. They are certainly a powerful tool that can be used in war today but the threat of using them may prevent tension from developing into all-out war. The Cold War was a period of tension that existed between the Soviet Bloc (including Russia) and Western countries (including the USA) from 1945 to 1991. Each side amassed large quantities of weapons, including nuclear bombs. The USA and the Soviet Union never fought directly, partly because if one side used nuclear weapons it would end in the complete destruction of both sides. The nuclear weapons were seen as a deterrent.

Figure 4.9 The explosion of the atomic bomb over Hiroshima in 1945

Benefits of WMD	Problems of WMD
• They offer a stronger and quicker method of winning a war. They give the side using WMD an advantage if the other side is unable to combat the use of such weapons.	• WMD are indiscriminate; they do not choose who they attack and who they avoid.
• WMD inflict great damage and destruction on the opposition but protect the side using them. Minimal losses will be incurred by those using WMD.	• The purpose of WMD is to cause as much destruction as possible, which means they harm civilians and buildings as well as the intended targets.
• The use of WMD in earlier wars brought an end to war and prevented further casualties. In WWII the USA used nuclear weapons in Japan, which helped bring the war to a close.	• There is a question over whether it is ever morally right to use WMD knowing how much damage and loss of life they can cause. Many people think that this type of weapon has no place in society today.
• The fear of the effect of using WMD may be enough to deter other nations from starting wars in the first place.	• Stockpiling WMD leads to other issues, such as finding appropriate sites to store them.
	• Questions have been asked about whether the use of WMD makes any war fair. Surely the side using WMD have an ultimate advantage that cannot be justified?
	• Conditions of Just War theory cannot be met using WMD which, for many, would make them unjustifiable to use in cases of war.

Islam and WMD

Islam teaches that Muslims should do everything they can to achieve peace before turning to war. The Qur'an advises that war can be fought as a last resort if the intention is to defend Islam against attack, but Muslims should not be the ones to start a conflict. The Qur'an was recorded centuries before WMD were created and there are no direct teachings on them. However, Muslims generally believe that the conditions of war set by Islam can be applied to WMD. This includes teachings such as war should be fought without killing innocent lives or damaging property and the environment.

From this perspective, the use of WMD would be unjustifiable due to the extensive damage they are capable of causing. This type of weapon would not be able to be regulated or accepted under Islamic conditions for war because the damage it could cause would always have the potential to be greater than anticipated.

What are non-religious attitudes towards the use of WMD?

Atheists do not believe in God and hold non-religious views on what is acceptable morally and what is not. They may hold similar views to those held by religious believers but for different reasons. Concerning WMD, many atheists see them as wrong due to the damage they are capable of causing. Most atheists believe human life is special, even though they do not accept the belief that this life came from a divine being, and would not support its destruction.

Sources of authority

When he turns his back, his aim everywhere is to spread mischief through the earth and destroy crops and cattle. But Allah loves not mischief. (Surah 2:205)

Activities

1   Do you think it is possible to justify the use of WMD? Make sure you can justify your opinion with reasons why you hold this view.

2   Write a conversation between a Muslim and a Humanist about the use of WMD. Make sure you include reasons for their beliefs.

3   Imagine you have been asked to represent the views of young people at a United Nations conference on the use of WMD. Interview your peers to find out their views on this topic and then write down what you would say to the people at the conference.

Humanists seek to live good lives without reference to religious beliefs. They instead value the use of reason, experience and respect when making decisions. Their views on war relate to their understanding of why human life is special. Humanists value life as they do not accept any sort of belief in an afterlife. They see the use of WMD as wrong because it threatens human life. Although they are not necessarily opposed to war they believe non-violent solutions should be sought first. The sheer scale of damage that weapons of mass destruction has the potential to cause goes against Humanist teachings. Despite Humanists and other atheists having a different perspective to Muslims, they do hold some views in common, namely that WMD would not be supported due to the high threat and cost of innocent life.

Ethical theories such as utilitarianism may hold that sometimes, for the greater benefit, WMD may be justified. If the outcome of using them would mean that larger groups of people are saved, this could be used as a suitable justification. Some non-religious people may share this view as well. Muslims, however, would respond to these views by maintaining that any loss of life is not justified by the saving of others. They recognise that all human life is sacred and special as it was created by Allah.

Exam-style question

In this question, 3 of the marks awarded will be for your spelling, punctuation and grammar and your use of specialist terminology.

'There is never any justification for fighting wars using weapons of mass destruction.'

Evaluate this statement considering arguments for and against. In your responses you should refer to Muslim teachings and reach a justified conclusion. **(15 marks)**

Exam tip

You are asked to consider different views on this statement. Consider what a Muslim would say as well as a contrasting view, such as a Humanist. Remember that different people can hold the same view but for differing reasons, so show awareness of this in your answer.

Summary

- Weapons of mass destruction are nuclear, biological or chemical weapons that are designed to cause widespread damage and threat to life.
- There are advantages and disadvantages in using weapons of mass destruction.
- Many people do not support the use of weapons of mass destruction due to their destructive nature.
- Muslims do not support the use of weapons of mass destruction as they go against the conditions of war set by Islam in the Qur'an.
- Humanists and many other atheists do not support the use of weapons of mass destruction as they believe life is special and should not be threatened.

Checkpoint

Strengthen

S1 What is a weapon of mass destruction?

S2 What are the benefits and disadvantages of using weapons of mass destruction?

S3 What do Muslims, Humanists and other atheists believe about the use of weapons of mass destruction?

Challenge

C1 Why do you think Muslims, Humanists and other atheists may hold similar views about weapons of mass destruction?

C2 Do you think the use of weapons of mass destruction can ever be justified?

C3 What do you think should be done about countries that currently have weapons of mass destruction?

4.8 Issues surrounding conflict

Learning objectives

- To understand the nature and history of problems involved in conflict.
- To consider Muslim views on the issues surrounding conflict and how Muslims have worked to overcome them.
- To explore non-religious views on issues surrounding conflict.

Nature and history of problems involved in conflict

Conflict is not a new idea and it takes different forms. At one level, there are examples of bullying in schools or workplaces, where a person intimidates or hurts another. At another level, conflict occurs between larger groups of people within or between countries where it becomes war.

Although the issues over why people go to war have changed very little, the way that wars are fought have changed dramatically. Violence, war and terrorism are more apparent today than in any other time in history. The use of technology means that new weapons and forms of warfare are becoming more and more sophisticated. This knowledge means that people are more able to use violent methods in fighting others, which are designed to cause maximum pain and suffering and gain advantage over the enemy. Knowledge of the world also means that targets can be identified more easily in conflict. Wars today are very different from the hand-to-hand combat of the time of Muhammad. They are fought on larger geographical areas with the use of aircraft, ships and tanks. Developments in weapons rapidly increased in the Second World War with the use of the atomic bomb. New technology means wars can be fought on a much larger scale and remotely from battlefields. For example, unmanned aircraft can be controlled by computers to take bombs into inaccessible areas to attack enemies.

Terrorism

Terrorism has long been associated with religion but the suicide attacks of 11 September 2001 in New York in America saw the threat of terrorism taken to a new level. Since then, the threat of terrorism has expanded globally with suicide bombers targeting cities all over the world, such as London, Paris, Mumbai, Ankara and others, claiming to be performing actions in the name of Allah. The term 'Muslim' has seemed to become synonymous with 'terrorism' with the media perception and promotion of this idea fuelling this misconception.

This threat has led to a multitude of issues including **Islamophobia**, which is the prejudice of Islam and Muslims, discrimination, retaliation to attacks and fear. Although there is often an association made between the religion of Islam and the concept of terrorism, it must also be recognised that there are many examples of terrorism where religion has played no role. An example of this is Timothy McVeigh, whose politically-motivated attack in Oklahoma City in 1995 killed 184 people and injured over 600 but had no religious motivation.

Since terrorism became more associated with Islam after the attacks in America, there have been many occasions where both Muslims and non-Muslims have tried to promote the religion of Islam as a religion of peace. Muslims have spoken out through the media to challenge negative stereotypes of Islam, as well as opening Mosques to all people to improve understanding of the faith and provide the opportunity to find out more. Many organisations, such as Muslim Aid, have had a role in recognising Islam as a religion of peace through supporting events such as the International Day of Peace on 21 September, where they have promoted the true ideas of the religion.

Islam and views on conflict

Islam maintains that it is a religion of peace and that extremists who choose to carry out attacks on others in the name of Allah are not representing Islam. It is fair to say that Muslims have found it difficult to live in a changing world where their religion is associated with the actions of a minority of individuals who claim that attacking others is defence of Islam.

Many Muslims do not accept that war and conflict is the best option when conflict needs to be resolved. They see the use of warfare in defence of Islam as a last resort after all peaceful, non-violent methods have been exhausted. Islam teaches the importance of living in harmony with others and does not support the use of conflict in solving problems. However, as we have previously seen within this chapter, Islam does recognise that in some situations conflict may be required and indeed is advocated by sources of authority such as the Qur'an in order to defend the religion of Islam. This, therefore, shows that there may be diversity within the religion on the rightness or wrongness of conflict in resolving disputes.

The threat to Islam from terrorism has led to many examples of Muslims being treated badly. The media promoting ideas that Islam is a terrorist religion has led to Islamophobia, where many people in different countries fear those who follow the Islamic faith as they do not understand the religion fully. Muslims believe that the religion of Islam has been misrepresented through the actions of minorities who perform terrorist actions. Although it is impossible to deny that there are terrorists who claim to be Muslims, this is not a fair or true representation of the religion of Islam.

Non-religious views

Humanists respond to current conflict in the world by wanting to bring change, peace and an end to fighting. They believe it is important to offer alternatives to religion to try to bring harmony between people. Humanists believe human life is special and therefore will do what is necessary to protect it. They do not agree with conflict that happens in the world today and believe that peaceful solutions need to be found and promoted so that all people can live together in harmony. Muslims, again, hold some beliefs in common with Humanists and other atheists concerning conflict. They believe that, if possible, non-violent solutions should be sought in order

to maintain the ideas of life being special and that it shouldn't be threatened. Muslims would respond to non-religious views by upholding their shared belief that life is special and should be preserved.

> ### Sources of authority
>
> *Go you forth, (whether equipped) lightly or heavily, and strive and struggle, with your goods and your persons, in the Cause of Allah. That is best for you, if you (but) knew.* (Surah 9:41)

How have Muslims worked to overcome these issues?

Islamophobia, or the fear of Islam, has only recently been widely recognised, although it arguably has been happening for a long period of time. There have been recent examples of this, where Mosques have been attacked or damaged, discriminated against, or attacked or where they have faced abuse. To overcome this:

- Muslims believe they should follow instructions given to them in the Qur'an to use their money and wealth to overcome issues within the world and help others
- Muslims have tried to make the religion of Islam more open to those outside it by showing what it really means to be a Muslim. The Muslim Council of Britain has organised various events designed to try to educate the public about Islam. Mosques have been opened for people to visit and find out more about the religion, so they fear it less, as they are less ignorant of the true meaning of Islam
- Muslims have taken part in rallies and marches to try to raise awareness of Islam and support peace
- interfaith groups have been established to try to bring harmony and unity between different faith groups. These include All Faiths Network and the Christian Muslim Forum. The Muslim Council of Britain has also holds a role in working to develop interfaith relationships. They all promote ideas of mutual respect and working together
- Muslim representatives have met with the police to work out a plan of action to protect Muslims when they face threats from Islamophobia
- there have also been charity initiatives such as the work of Mosaic, founded by the Prince of Wales, to challenge ideas of Islamophobia
- Muslims may also look to Hadith for guidance on what they can do to overcome issues of conflict within the world. An important source of authority is Malik's Muwatta, which is in the Source of authority box.

Figure 4.10 The Muslim Council of Britain works to promote peace

Sources of authority

Yahya related to me from Malik from Yahya ibn Said that Abu Bakr as-Siddiq was sending armies to ash-Sham. He went for a walk with Yazid ibn Abi Sufyan who was the commander of one of the battalions. It is claimed that Yazid said to Abu Bakr, "Will you ride or shall I get down?" Abu Bakrsaid, "I will not ride and you will not get down. I intend these steps of mine to be in the way of Allah."

Then Abu Bakr advised Yazid, "You will find a people who claim to have totally given themselves to Allah. Leave them to what they claim to have given themselves. You will find a people who have shaved the middle of their heads, strike what they have shaved with the sword.

"I advise you ten things: Do not kill women or children or an aged, infirm person. Do not cut down fruit-bearing trees. Do not destroy an inhabited place. Do not slaughter sheep or camels except for food. Do not burn bees and do not scatter them. Do not steal from the booty, and do not be cowardly." (Imam Malik's Muwatta, 21.3.10)

Activities

1 Imagine you have the opportunity to make changes to today's world which will improve fairness in society and challenge some of the injustices that exist. Write down five things that you would want to change and give a reason to explain each one.

2 In pairs, consider the following statement and create a list of arguments to agree with it and arguments to disagree with it: 'We should all do more to bring an end to conflict in the world today.'

3 Write a response to the following question: 'Do you think good can ever come out of conflict?' Make sure you explain at least three reasons for your opinion.

Exam-style question

In this question, 3 of the marks awarded will be for your spelling, punctuation and grammar and your use of specialist terminology.
'We will never end conflict in today's world.'
Evaluate this statement, considering arguments for and against. In your responses you should refer to Muslim teachings and reach a justified conclusion. **(15 marks)**

Exam tip

This question requires you to consider a range of different views so make sure you do this within your answer. Think carefully about how a Muslim would respond to this statement and make sure you explain fully why they would believe this.

Summary

- The nature of war and conflict has changed in the modern world.
- Terrorism is a growing problem in society today.
- The threat of terrorism has led to the growth of Islamophobia and many Muslims being the targets of abuse.
- Many actions have been used to try and combat Islamophobia.
- Humanists and many other atheists believe that conflict in today's world needs to be overcome.

Checkpoint

Strengthen

S1 What issues has conflict brought to today's world?

S2 How do Muslims respond and work to overcome issues of conflict in today's world?

S3 What do Humanists and many other atheists think about conflict in today's world?

Challenge

C1 Do you think it is actually possible to bring an end to conflict in today's world?

C2 How does conflict in today's world not support Islamic ideas of a just society?

C3 Do you think the biggest threat to the world today is terrorism?

Recap: Peace and conflict

Use the activities and exam-style questions on the following pages to reinforce your learning before you move on to the next chapter.

Recap quiz

Muslim attitudes towards peace

1 What is peace?
2 Why is peace important for Muslims?
3 How is Islam seen as a religion of peace?
4 How are ideas of peace associated with Allah?

Muslims and peacemaking

5 Why do Muslims believe justice, forgiveness and reconciliation are important in peacemaking?
6 How are ideas of peace associated with Allah?
7 Why do Muslims believe in ideas of justice?
8 What does the Qur'an teach about justice?
9 What have Muslims done to try to work for peace?
10 Name an Islamic organisation that has worked for peace.

Muslim attitudes to conflict

11 What are the causes of conflict in society?
12 How do Muslims respond to the causes of conflict in society?
13 Why do Muslims believe it is important to work for peace for Allah?
14 What does Islam teach about the way Muslims should treat others?

Pacifism

15 What is pacifism?
16 Why is Islam not a pacifist religion?
17 What is passive resistance?
18 What does Islam teach about passive resistance?
19 How are ideas about 'submission to Allah' seen within Islamic ideas about war and peace?

Just War theory

20 What is Just War theory?
21 What are the conditions that need to be met for a just war?
22 What do Muslims believe about Just War theory?

Holy war

23 What is Harb al-Maqadis?
24 What are the Islamic conditions for Harb al-Maqadis?

Weapons of mass destruction

25 What are weapons of mass destruction?
26 What are the benefits and problems of using weapons of mass destruction?
27 What do Muslims believe about the use of weapons of mass destruction?
28 What do Humanists and other atheists believe about the use of weapons of mass destruction?

Issues surrounding conflict

29 What conflict problems are faced by the world today?
30 What do Muslims believe about conflict in the world today?
31 Why do Muslims believe it is important to remember past events in the history of Islam?
32 What do Humanists and many other atheists believe about conflict in the world today?

Activities ?

1   Make a list of any new terms you have come across in this chapter. Create some flashcards to help you remember what they mean.

2   Create a bullet-point list of the 10 most important things you have learned about Islam and Muslim beliefs about peace and conflict from this chapter.

3   In groups, role play an interview between a Muslim, a person from another faith and a Humanist about their beliefs on peace and conflict. Make sure you stay in character while discussing beliefs about this topic and use arguments to support views that you include.

4   Write a 150-word press release explaining the Muslim view on war and peace.

5   In pairs, explain whether you agree with each of the following statements. Then imagine you are a Muslim and discuss what your response would be:

'War is always wrong.'

'Life is so important that war should be banned.'

'There is nothing I can do to bring peace to the world.'

'Everyone should be able to live together peacefully in the world.'

6   Make a list of three things you would want to change in the world. Then make a list of what you believe needs to be done in order to achieve them. Write a speech explaining these, trying to persuade others that they should elect you to rule the world and bring about these changes.

Exam questions

- Outline three Muslim beliefs about conflict. **(3 marks)**

- Explain two features of Just War theory for Muslims. **(4 marks)**

- Explain two reasons why peace is important in Islam. In your response you must refer to a source of wisdom or authority. **(5 marks)**

- In this question, 3 of the marks awarded will be for your spelling, punctuation and grammar and your use of specialist terminology.
  'We all have a responsibility to try and bring peace to the world.' Evaluate this statement, considering arguments for and against. In your response you should refer to Muslim teachings and reach a justified conclusion.
  (15 marks)

Exam tips

- Make sure you read the question carefully so you are clear on what it is asking you to do in your answer.

- Always take time to consider what knowledge you want to demonstrate in your answer.

- Make sure for longer answers you explain ideas fully and develop each point you make by using examples, evidence and quotes where possible.

- Make sure you always check through your answers once complete.

- When giving different views, make sure you support each one with at least two different reasons.

- Remember that you have to demonstrate your knowledge and show you understand how ideas are related to each other in your work. Remember to return to your prior knowledge and topics you have covered in other chapters to do this.

- Make sure that when you are trying to persuade people of your view that it is important to use persuasive language. You need to always check that what you have written suits the purpose it is intended for.

Extend: Peace and conflict

Source

The following four people live in different places across the world. They are asking for help and support to go to war.

1 Tahseen

I live in a small remote village and my house has been attacked. Last night, thieves came into my house and took my belongings. They also took some of my animals. My family were asleep and we didn't hear them but they could have attacked us too. They are very dangerous and must be stopped. I expect they are from the next village. We should get a group together and fight them. We have to stop them doing this to other innocent people.

2 Fatima

My village needs your help. A group of religious extremists have settled at the edge of our village. They seem to have money and are trying to tempt people in my village away from Islam. They are targeting young people who may be more impressionable and think that they can offer a better life for them. Some youngsters have already left with them. We have tried to talk to them but it's as though they are brainwashing them. What can we do? We need support from the ummah to try to stop this happening. Our religion and lives are being attacked and the only correct action is to go to war.

3 Abaan

I need help. I have travelled a long distance to let you know that our country is under attack. I have seen tanks and weapons on the hills to the north. They seem to be heavily armed and ready to try to take our country by force. We are in great danger. If they attack, we won't stand a chance unless we are united. We need to stand together and firm to stand up to this injustice.

4 Aisha

I live in an Islamic country where Shari'ah law is used to rule. My family and I, as well as the people in my village, are being threatened by those in power. They expect us to do exactly as they say and punish us if we don't. However, when we need help they don't come to our aid. When we need food or clean water, where are they? It's time for us to try to do something about the situation. We must gather all the people who can fight and stand up against this government who don't help us. We need to have our voices heard.

Activities ?

1. Write down in your own words what dilemma each person is facing concerning peace, war and conflict.

2. Using your knowledge of Islam, make a list of any teachings from the Qur'an that could be used to help each person understand what Islam teaches about their situation.

3. Imagine you are a Muslim who has been asked to respond to each person. Using Islamic teachings, what advice would you give to each person about what Islam says about their situation? Would it be right for them to go to war? Why or why not?

4. In groups, role play each scenario and try to persuade the rest of the class that you have the strongest case to go to war. As a class, vote on whether you would support them. Would a Muslim say the same thing? Why or why not?

5. Consider each of the following statements and debate them as a class:

   • 'Islam is out of date when looking at issues about peace and conflict in today's world.'

   • 'Everyone in the world should support ideas of pacifism.'

   • 'Just War theory is no help when making a decision about going to war.'

   • 'There is too much conflict in today's world for us to ever have peace.'

Exam tips

• Always make sure you explain your answer fully, giving as much detail as possible.

• Take care with your spelling, especially with Islamic terms.

• Make sure that when you are asked to offer different views that you show why their opinions may differ and include sufficient reasons to show you understand their views.

Can you remember?

• What conditions do Muslims believe must be met before war is the accepted option?

• Why do Muslims believe war should only be a last resort?

• What do Muslims believe about submitting to Allah in everything they do?

• What sources of authority do Muslims refer to when exploring issues such as peace and conflict?

• What do Muslims believe about life after death and how might this impact on their beliefs about peace and conflict?

Preparing for your GCSE Islam Paper 2 exam

In specification B, the exam has three papers covering three areas of study, from which you choose two. The papers are:

- Paper 1: Religion and ethics
- Paper 2: Religion, peace and conflict
- Paper 3: Religion, philosophy and social justice.

The exam for Paper 2 on Religion, peace and conflict will last for 1 hour and 45 minutes (105 minutes). It will count for 50% of the full GCSE qualification. In your exam you will be asked to respond to questions which relate to the topics you have studied in this book. These are listed below.

The remaining 50% of the GCSE qualification will come from the study of a different religion. You will be examined on, for example, Christianity in either Paper 1 or Paper 3, depending on the topics that have been chosen by your school. The topics for Christianity Paper 1 and Paper 3 are listed on page 128, demonstrating the overall topic structure that is echoed across each of the religions available to study.

Islam Paper 2: Religion, peace and conflict

Muslim beliefs

- [ ] The Six Beliefs of Islam
  - their nature, history and purpose
  - their importance
  - how they are understood today
- [ ] The Five Roots of 'Usul ad-Din in Shi'a Islam
  - their nature, history and purpose
  - their importance
- [ ] The nature of Allah
  - what Muslims believe about Allah
  - how Allah is described in the Qur'an
  - why this is important to Muslims
- [ ] Risalah: prophethood
  - the nature and importance of prophethood
  - what Muslims learn from the prophets
  - the examples of Adam, Ibrahim, Isma'il, Musa, Dawud, Isa and Muhammad
- [ ] Muslim holy books – kutub
  - their nature and history
  - their significance
  - their importance and purpose today
- [ ] Malaikah: angels
  - their nature and importance
  - how Jibril, Izra'il and Mika'il are shown in the Qur'an
  - the significance of angels today

- [ ] Al-Qadr: predestination
  - its nature and importance
  - how it relates to the Day of Judgement
  - what it means for Muslims today
- [ ] Akhirah: life after death
  - Muslim teachings about Akhirah
  - judgement, paradise and hell
  - how Akhirah affects Muslims' daily life

Living the Muslim life

- [ ] Ten Obligatory Acts of Shi'a Islam
  - their nature, history and purpose
  - how they are practised today
  - why they are important today
- [ ] Shahadah as one of the Five Pillars
  - its nature and role
  - its significance
  - why it is important for Muslims today
- [ ] Salah as one of the Five Pillars
  - its nature, history and significance
  - how it is performed
  - prayer in the mosque and at home
- [ ] Sawm as one of the Five Pillars
  - its nature, role, significance and purpose
  - who is excused from fasting and why

- the nature, history, significance and purpose of Laylat al-Qadr
- why Laylat al-Qadr is important today

☐ Zakah as one of the Five Pillars and Khums
  - the nature, role, significance and purpose of Zakah and Khums
  - why Zakah is important for Sunnis and Khums is important for Shi'a Muslims
  - the benefits of Khums

☐ Hajj as one of the Five Pillars
  - its nature, role, origins and significance
  - how it is performed and why it is important
  - its benefits and challenges

☐ Jihad
  - its origins, meaning and significance
  - greater and lesser jihad
  - the conditions needed for lesser jihad
  - the importance of jihad

☐ Celebrations and commemorations
  - the nature and origins of Id-ul-Adha and Id-ul-Fitr in Sunni Islam
  - the nature and origins of Id-ul-Ghadeer and Ashura in Shi'a Islam
  - their significance

Crime and punishment

☐ Justice
  - the nature and importance of justice
  - why it is important for the victim

☐ Crime
  - the nature of crime and why it occurs
  - what actions Muslims can take to end the causes of crime

☐ Good, evil and suffering
  - Islamic teachings about good and evil
  - the rewards and punishments of good and evil actions
  - Muslim beliefs about why people suffer

☐ Punishment
  - the nature and importance of punishment
  - Qur'anic teachings about punishment
  - why punishment may be just and why it may be needed

☐ The aims of punishment
  - the Muslim response to the aims of punishment
  - strengths and weaknesses
  - Qur'anic teachings on punishment

☐ Forgiveness
  - the nature of forgiveness
  - how the community may forgive offenders
  - restorative justice and why it is important

☐ The treatment of criminals
  - Muslim beliefs on how criminals should be treated
  - atheist and Humanist views on the treatment of criminals

☐ Capital punishment
  - its nature and purpose
  - Muslim views on the death penalty
  - atheist and Humanist views on the death penalty

Peace and conflict

☐ Muslim attitudes towards peace
  - its nature and importance for Muslims
  - Muslim teachings on peace
  - why Islam is a religion of peace

☐ Muslims and peacemaking
  - Muslim teachings on peacemaking
  - justice, forgiveness and reconciliation
  - Muslims working for peace today

☐ Muslim attitudes to conflict
  - the nature and causes of conflict
  - social problems caused by conflict
  - Muslim responses to the causes of conflict

☐ Pacifism
  - its nature and history
  - Muslim teachings on passive resistance
  - how Muslims use passive resistance

☐ Just War theory
  - its nature, history and importance
  - whether Just War is possible
  - Muslim teachings on Just War

☐ Holy War
  - the nature of Holy War
  - Qur'anic teachings on war and peace
  - Muslim teachings on war

☐ Weapons of mass destruction
  - problems and benefits
  - Muslim attitudes
  - atheist and Humanist views

☐ Issues surrounding conflict
  - its nature and history
  - Muslim views and efforts to overcome problems
  - atheist and Humanist views

Preparing for your exam

Choose **either** Paper 1 **or** Paper 2 in your second religion, for example Christianity.

Christianity Paper 1: Religion and ethics

Christian beliefs

- [ ] The Trinity
- [ ] The creation of the universe and of humanity
- [ ] The Incarnation
- [ ] The last days of Jesus' life
- [ ] Atonement and salvation
- [ ] Christian eschatology
- [ ] The problem of evil/suffering and a loving and righteous God
- [ ] Divergent solutions offered to the problem of evil/suffering and a loving and righteous God

Living the Christian life

- [ ] Christian worship
- [ ] The role of the sacraments
- [ ] Prayer
- [ ] Pilgrimage
- [ ] Religious celebrations
- [ ] The Church and local communities
- [ ] The worldwide Church and its future

Marriage and the family

- [ ] Marriage
- [ ] Sexual relationships
- [ ] The importance of family
- [ ] Support for the family in the local parish
- [ ] Contraception and family planning
- [ ] Divorce
- [ ] Equality of men and women in the family
- [ ] Gender prejudice and discrimination

Matters of life and death

- [ ] The origins and value of the universe
- [ ] The sanctity of life
- [ ] The origins and value of human life
- [ ] Abortion
- [ ] Belief in life after death
- [ ] Christian responses to arguments against life after death
- [ ] Euthanasia
- [ ] Animal rights and the natural world

Christianity Paper 3: Religion, philosophy and social justice

Christian beliefs

- [ ] The Trinity
- [ ] The creation of the universe and of humanity
- [ ] The Incarnation
- [ ] The last days of Jesus' life
- [ ] The nature and significance of salvation and the role of Christ within salvation
- [ ] Christian eschatology
- [ ] The problem of evil/suffering and a loving and righteous God
- [ ] Divergent solutions offered to the problem of evil/suffering and a loving and righteous God

Philosophy of Religion

- [ ] Revelation
- [ ] Visions
- [ ] Miracles
- [ ] Christian attitudes towards religious experiences
- [ ] The design argument
- [ ] The cosmological argument
- [ ] Religious upbringing

Living the Christian life

- [ ] Christian worship
- [ ] The role of the sacraments
- [ ] Prayer
- [ ] Pilgrimage
- [ ] Religious celebrations
- [ ] The future of the Church
- [ ] The Church and local communities
- [ ] The Church and the worldwide community
- [ ] Equality
- [ ] Human rights

Equality

- [ ] Religious freedom
- [ ] Prejudice and discrimination
- [ ] Racial harmony
- [ ] Racial discrimination
- [ ] Social justice
- [ ] Wealth and poverty

Preparing for your exam

The questions

In the exam for Paper 2 you will be asked to answer four questions in writing. These will be on each of the chapters you have studied:

- Muslim beliefs
- Living the Muslim life
- Crime and punishment
- Peace and conflict

Each of the four questions, numbered 1 to 4, has a number of parts: a), b), c) and d). Each part carries different marks. You must answer all the parts of a question in order to gain the most marks.

The following is an example of a *complete* exam question based on Chapter 2, Living the Muslim Life:

1 a) Outline three of the Ten Obligatory Acts of Shi'a Islam.

(3 marks)

b) Explain two reasons why Muslims may differ in the way they help the poor.

(4 marks)

c) Explain two reasons why the Night of Power is important for Muslims. In your answer must refer to a source of wisdom and authority.

(5 marks)

d) 'Shahadah is the most important of the Five Pillars.' Evaluate this statement considering arguments for and against. In your response you should:
  – refer to Muslim teachings
  – refer to different Muslim points of view
  – reach a justified conclusion.

(12 marks)

Total = 24 marks

Exam tips

Remember that you must try to answer all parts (a–d) of each of the four questions.

Question types

The paper is likely to include a combination of short open response, open response and extended writing questions.

Typically, part a) and b) questions will ask you to outline or explain something. These are examples of short open response questions.

Open response (part c), and extended writing questions (part d) will carry the most marks. This is because you are expected to provide more detailed responses. You should also include a reference to a source of wisdom and authority, such as a quote from the Qur'an, in part c) and often in part d) questions.

In **open response questions** you can choose what information to include, depending on which points you think are most relevant to the question.

Extended writing questions are also open response questions, but they are a longer and more developed piece of writing which discusses issues in more depth and comes to a conclusion.

Mark scheme

- You will be awarded up to 3 marks for a correct answer to part a) questions.
- You will be awarded up to 4 marks for a correct answer to part b) questions.
- You will be awarded up to 5 marks for a correct answer to part c) questions.
- You will be awarded up to 12 marks for a correct answer to part d) questions.

Exam tips

- Try to learn specialist terminology as you go along.
- The marks for each question <u>or</u> part of each question are shown in brackets at the end of the question. Use them as a rough guide for how much time to spend on a question. For example:
  - 3 minutes on a part a) 3-mark question.
  - 4 minutes on a part b) 4-mark question.
  - 5 minutes on a part c) 5-mark question.
  - 12 minutes on a part d) 12- or 15-mark question.
- You should also take a minute to check your spelling, punctuation and grammar if it is a 15-mark question.

In two out of the four part d) questions you will be awarded up to 3 additional marks for your spelling, punctuation, grammar (SPaG) and your use of specialist terminology. This means that some part d) questions will be worth a maximum of 15 marks.

'Specialist terminology' means the specific key words and phrases associated with the issue that the question is focused on. For example, *annulment* is an example of specialist terminology that you might use when discussing the issue of divorce. Specialist terminology is highlighted in bold type for you throughout the book, and definitions are given in the glossary on pages 140–142.

Paper 2 is worth a total of 102 marks. The breakdown of marks across the four complete questions, including marks for SPaG and use of specialist terminology, is as follows:

- Question 1 is worth a maximum of 27 marks
- Question 2 is worth a maximum of 24 marks
- Question 3 is worth a maximum of 27 marks
- Question 4 is worth a maximum of 24 marks.

Examiners will mark your answers according to a mark scheme. The mark scheme has two assessment objectives: AO1 and AO2.

Assessment Objective 1

Assessment Objective 1 (AO1) focuses on your ability to demonstrate your knowledge and understanding of Islam. This means that an examiner will be reading what you have written and assessing what you know about:

- Muslim beliefs, practices and sources of authority, such as what Muslims believe, what they base those beliefs on, and what attitudes they have and how they act as a result of those beliefs.
- the influence of Muslim beliefs on individuals, communities and societies, such as the impact that Muslim beliefs have on the lives of individual Muslims, their local communities and the world.
- the similarities and differences within and/or between individual Muslims and Muslim groups, such as the way individual Muslims or different parts of the Muslim community can believe and practise different things, even though they are all part of the same religion.

Assessment Objective 2

Assessment Objective 2 (AO2) focuses on your ability to analyse and evaluate aspects of Islam and Muslim beliefs. You will need to show that you can communicate different points of view using reasons and evidence, on topics including:

- the influence and significance of Islam and Muslim beliefs, such as the importance of Islam and Muslim beliefs and the meaning and impact they might have on the lives of individual Muslims, the Muslim community and the wider society in which the Muslim community exists
- your ability to make connections between different aspects of Muslim beliefs
- your ability to use evidence from what you have learned to reach a justified conclusion in the part d) questions.

Revision strategy

The key to success in exams often lies in good planning. Make sure you know what you need to do and when you need to do it. **Start early by making the most of your lessons!** The more you understand, learn and practise as you go along, the less intensive revision you will need to do.

Try to make sure that you always understand everything you have been taught. Most importantly, ask for help or clarification if you need it. Take every opportunity to put your learning into practice throughout the GCSE course by doing the activities and practice exam-style questions in this book. Taking part in class discussions is also an excellent way of developing your learning.

Planning your revision time

Make sure you know what revision strategies work best for you in this subject. It is also important that you are realistic about how much time you have for revision and how much you can fit into one revision session. Planning a revision timetable well in advance of your exams can help with this.

Exam tips

Break up your revision into smaller chunks. This will make it more manageable.

Everyone is different, but 'a little and often' is thought to be best way to tackle revision – perhaps revising one or two connected topics at a time. A thorough programme of revision is essential if you are to do well in your exams.

Know your strengths

Analyse your strengths and the areas that you need to develop using your own insights and the feedback you get from your class teacher throughout the course. Try to address any gaps in your knowledge and understanding straight away. Don't avoid it because not understanding or knowing something could make it more difficult to learn other things in the future.

Exam tips

Remember to review your progress regularly as you work through the course. This will let you see where you have improved and what you still need to work on.

Activities ?

As you finish each topic, make a list of how well you know it. You can use the checklist on pages 126–127 to help. Try to identify areas that you know less about or don't understand, and use the book or ask your teacher or one of your classmates to help you improve. Don't forget to celebrate your strengths. These are a good foundation on which to build and develop your knowledge and understanding further.

Most importantly, have confidence in your ability to do well!

Get Connected!

The other important thing to do is to **make connections between the things you have learned**. This will make the information much easier to remember and help you to revise more efficiently. The diagram below shows how different aspects of Islam can be connected.

Making connections is easy! Start with a key Muslim belief about God and get connected. What connections can you make between things that you have learned?

In groups, each pick a different belief about Allah from Chapter 1 and draw a 'get connected' diagram to share with the group. Use the chapter and topic summary at the beginning of this section or the more detailed checklist at the end of the book to help you.

> The Muslim belief in Tawhid, the one-ness of Allah, is connected to the belief that Allah alone had the power to create the universe.

> This belief that Allah created the universes demonstrates that Allah is all-powerful and has control over everything that exists. This belief is connected to the respect and obedience that Muslims believe they owe to Allah as their creator and sustainer.

> It is also connected to the belief that all life is sacred and has value because it has been created by Allah and this connects to Muslim attitudes and beliefs about matters of life and death, such as abortion and euthanasia. There is a connection also to the Muslim belief in the ummah, the unity of all Muslims, and in the equality of all people, regardless of race, religion or gender.

> A connection can be made between Muslim beliefs about the creation of the universe and Muslim attitudes towards the natural world and their duty to protect the environment.

Understanding the question

It is important that you understand exactly what it is that you are being asked to do when answering a question. Read every question carefully at least twice. Pay attention to the number of marks and the command words. As mentioned previously, the number of marks gives you an idea of how many minutes you should spend answering the question.

Command words

Each question will contain a command word. Command words are important because they tell you how you should respond to the question and what the examiner is asking you to do. The command words that you are likely to find in the exam paper are:

- Outline
- State
- Describe
- Explain
- Evaluate

Exam tips

Question c) is asking you to give details about Muslim beliefs about angels and why this belief is important for Muslims. You need to write about the role of angels in Islam and how Allah uses angels in his relations with human beings, together with an explanation, for example, of how angels influenced the life of Muhammad and how they might influence the lives of Muslims today. You must include a source, such as a quotation from the Qur'an, that supports your explanation.

In addition to command words, questions will contain other information that can help you to answer them correctly. For example, in the following questions, useful words that tell you what to write about have been underlined.

c) **Explain** two reasons why _belief in angels is important_ for Muslims.
In your answer you must refer to a source of wisdom and authority.

(5 marks)

d) 'The Muslim _belief in Predestination (al-Qadr)_ means that there is no such thing as _free will_.'
Evaluate this statement, considering arguments for and against.
In your response you should:
– refer to Muslim teachings
– refer to different Muslim points of view
– reach a justified conclusion.

(12 marks)

Exam tips

Question d) is asking you to weigh up (evaluate) whether or not this statement is true from the point of view of Muslim teaching. You would need to write about the Muslim view of Predestination (what it means and involves). It is also asking you whether all Muslims agree that this belief means that there is no such thing as free will. In order to support your argument, you would also need to consider whether some Muslims would say that it is possible for human beings to be predestined and still have the ability to make choices about how to live their lives. Lastly, a conclusion is needed, summarising your evaluation of this issue.

Answering the question

With a good plan, you should be able to answer the questions with no problems. On the following pages, there are examples of answers to exam-style questions. The questions have been unpicked for you and the command words are discussed.

Plan your answer

It's a good idea to plan your answer before you start writing it. Once you have understood what the question is asking, take a minute to think about how you want to respond. Ask yourself:

- What is the question asking me to do: outline, state, describe, explain or evaluate?
- What does the wording of the question say it is about?
- What key points do I need to make?
- How many points do I need to make?
- How many points do I need to make and develop?
- What specialist terminology should I use?
- Do I need to include more than one point of view?
- Will I need to put forward arguments and provide evidence to support them?
- Do I need a conclusion?

Keep focused

Make sure you know what you are going to say before you start writing. Have a plan for the structure and content of your response. Take a minute to write down a few bullet points or words about the information you are going to put in your answer, covering the order in which you are going to write your points and the specialist terminology you need to include. Try to tick off each point as you go, particularly for questions that require a longer answer. This will help you to stay focused on the question and not write about something irrelevant. You have enough time in the examination to answer each question correctly, provided you don't stray off the point.

Check your answer

Always try to read back through everything you have written, to check that it makes sense and says what you wanted it to. The examiner will award you marks on the basis of what you have actually written, not what you meant to write.

Make sure your handwriting is clear and easy to read. It does not need to be perfect, but the examiner must be able to read it! They will not be able to give you marks for something they cannot read properly. Poor handwriting can also affect the clarity of what you are trying to say in your responses.

Activities ?

1. Pick an answer that you wrote to one of the questions in the first chapter of the book. Review it against the example answers and list three things that you could improve about it.

2. In pairs or small groups, choose a part d) exam-style question from the book and create a plan for how to answer it. Think about how you want to structure your response as well as what you want to say.

3. Swap an answer that you've written previously with someone else in your class. Give each other helpful ideas about how it could be made better, or what might have been done differently. Then compare your answers.

Islam Paper 2, part a)

a) Outline three ways in which Muslims show respect to the Qur'an. **(3 marks)**

Exam tips

- Always use capital letters to begin sentences and for proper nouns (names), including 'God' or 'Allah'.

- Do not write in capitals. Use the correct combination of capitals and lower-case letters throughout your work.

Sample answer 1

Muslims show respect for the Qur'an by not eating when reading it, by not allowing the Qur'an to touch the ground, and by washing.

If a question is asking you to outline something, it is asking you to show your knowledge of Islam and Muslim beliefs by recalling factual information you have learned. These types of questions are usually worth 3 marks. You will normally be expected to make three separate points and can be awarded 1 mark for each correct point that you make.

Verdict – needs developing

- The first two ways mentioned have enough detail to gain marks.
- The third way – 'by washing' – does not fully describe what is involved or how that is a mark of respect.

Sample answer 2

Muslims show respect for the Qur'an by washing themselves before they touch it to make sure they are clean. They also do not eat or drink anything when reading the words of Allah. They do not allow the Qur'an to touch the ground so that it does not get dirty, but instead place it on a special cushion when it is being read.

The answers do not have to be long, but it is important to give enough detail to answer the question fully.

Verdict – strong

- Three ways are clearly described.
- The descriptions are complete, indicating the action and how it shows respect for the Qur'an.

Islam Paper 2, part b)

b) Explain two differences between Muslim and Christian beliefs about the oneness of God.   **(4 marks)**

Exam tips

- The way you present you work in examinations is important. Write clearly and try to avoid crossings out.

- Always write in full sentences. Do not use text-messaging or online chat abbreviations.

Sample answer 1

The Qur'an teaches that Allah has no partners. Christians believe that God is a Trinity of three persons.

If a question asks you to explain something, it is asking you to show your knowledge of a particular aspect of Islam by recalling factual information and developing it. You will normally be expected to make and develop two separate points. There are a maximum of 2 marks that can be awarded for each separate point.

Verdict – needs developing

- A difference between Muslim and Christian beliefs is explained.
- Two contrasting beliefs are explained simply.
- A second example of a difference in belief is needed to gain full marks.

Sample answer 2

The Qur'an teaches that Allah is indivisible and therefore has no partners, whereas Christians are also monotheists but believe that God is a Trinity of three persons. Muslims believe that Allah has never taken on any human form because they believe that God cannot be mortal, but many Christians believe that Jesus of Nazareth is also the Son of God, with the same substance as God the Father.

Always give two differences, and do not just state them – explain the difference between them.

Verdict – strong

- Two differences between Muslim and Christian beliefs are explained.
- The answer demonstrates a sophisticated and accurate understanding of two different theological approaches.

Islam Paper 2, part c)

c) Explain two reasons why the Prophet Muhammad is important for Muslims.
In your answer you must refer to a source of wisdom and authority.

(5 marks)

Exam tips

- What you choose to leave out of a question can be just as important as what you decide to include. Choose arguments that you know you can support with evidence.

- Use paragraphs to help structure your work. You should have a new paragraph for every key idea or point that you are making and developing.

Sample answer 1

Muslims believe Allah chose Muhammad to be his messenger, and that the words he preached were those revealed directly to him by Allah himself. Muslims believe that Muhammad is the seal of the prophets.

Verdict – needs developing

- Two valid reasons are given but only one of them is developed.
- The second reason is not developed.
- There is no reference to a source of wisdom and authority as required by the question.
- The answer uses the phrase 'seal of the prophets', but there is no sign that the student understands what this means.

Sample answer 2

Muslims believe that Allah chose Muhammad as his messenger, and the words he preached were those revealed directly to him by Allah himself. This is recorded in the Qur'an, where it says 'Allah knows best with whom to place his message'. Muslims also believe that Muhammad is the seal of the prophets, which means that he is the final prophet and his message overrides those of the prophets who came before him.

The source of wisdom and authority needs to relate directly to the question.

Verdict – strong

- There are two valid reasons why the prophet Muhammad is important to Muslims.
- Both reasons are developed.
- The answer gives a clear reference to a source of wisdom and authority by quoting from the Qur'an.

Islam Paper 2, part d)

In this question, 3 of the marks awarded will be for your spelling, punctuation and grammar and your use of specialist terminology.

d) 'Belief in the rewards of the afterlife is what guides the lives of Muslims.'
Evaluate this statement considering arguments for and against.
- In your response you should:
- refer to Muslim teachings
- refer to different Muslim point of view
- reach a justified conclusion.

(15 marks)

Exam tips

- Construct your sentences well. Make sure they are not too long. Use commas, colons and semicolons where appropriate and finish all of your sentences with a full stop.

Sample answer 1

Muslims believe that the soul continues to exist after death, and that their physical existence will be transformed. They also believe in a day of judgement when they will be sent to paradise or to hell, depending on their deeds in life. Therefore Muslims always try to live a good life and avoid sinning because they want to enjoy the pleasures of paradise as outlined in the Qur'an. Some Muslims say that the love of Allah is what is essential to being a Muslim, and that because of this love they try to live good lives.

If a question is asking you to evaluate something, it is asking you to look at different viewpoints, including your own, in relation to a particular issue and come to reasoned judgement on the matter in the form of a conclusion. You must refer to Islam, fully evaluate the issue and provide a thorough conclusion in order to gain the highest marks.

Verdict – needs developing

- The answer demonstrates an accurate understanding of Muslim religion and belief.
- There are two different Muslim responses.
- In one of the responses there is evidence of a logical chain of reasoning, but the alternative response is too brief and undeveloped.
- No attempt is made to draw a justified conclusion based on the arguments.
- Spelling, punctuation and grammar are accurate, but very few specialist terms have been used.

Islam Paper 2, part d)

d) 'Belief in the rewards of the afterlife is what guides the lives of Muslims.'
Evaluate this statement considering arguments for and against.

(15 marks)

Sample answer 2

Belief in life after death and the Day of Judgement is one of six fundamental beliefs that a Muslim requires to complete his faith. Muslims believe that the soul continues to exist after death and that their physical existence will be transformed. Because Muslims believe they will face judgement, when they will be sent to paradise or to hell, depending on their deeds in life, this is bound to be in the forefront of their minds when they decide how to behave. As it says in the Qur'an, Allah will be the reckoner on the day of judgement, that he will weigh people's deeds in a balance, allowing those whose good deeds outweigh their bad deeds into paradise. Therefore Muslims always try to live a good life and avoid sinning because they want to enjoy the pleasures of paradise as promised by Allah in the Qur'an.

However, many Muslims say that living a good life just for a reward can be selfish. This is an issue that is discussed by many of the major religions: whether doing good actions in the hope of reward, or to avoid punishment, is something to be praised. Many Muslim scholars agree that the love of Allah is what is most essential to being a good Muslim and that all the stages of human life that follow are fruits of that relationship with Allah. This also forms part of the spiritual jihad that all Muslims must fight, to conquer the inner battle between good and evil. Therefore it is because of this love, because they want to please Allah, that they try to live good lives in accordance with his will.

The religious meaning of the word 'Islam' is 'submission to the will of Allah'. Although I agree that Muslim belief in reward and punishment in the afterlife is important, it seems clear that the love of Allah, and submission to his will, is the very heart of Islam. For that reason we can say that Muslims' lives are guided less by the hope of paradise after they die, and more by the desire to show love for Allah in this life.

Exam tips

- In extended answer questions, make sure that you always express your own views in a balanced and measured way. Ensure that you link your views to the statement and other ideas that you have written about.

Verdict – strong

- The answer demonstrates a sustained and accurate understanding of Muslim religion and belief.
- There are two different Muslim points of view that respond directly to the question.
- In both responses there is evidence of a logical chain of reasoning that connects all the elements in the question.
- The essay highlights a major theological debate that is common to many religions.
- A clear attempt is made to draw a justified conclusion based on the arguments.
- Spelling, punctuation and grammar are accurate and specialist terms such as 'spiritual jihad' are used appropriately.

Glossary

Abrahamic religions that trace their roots back to the Prophet Abraham, such as Judaism, Christianity and Islam

Adalat the concept of Divine Justice, that Allah is fair and just

Adam first human being and prophet on Earth

adhan the call to prayer

ahimsa the practice of compassion and non-violence towards every living creature

Ali ibn abi talib cousin and son-in-law of Muhammad

al-Jannah the Islamic name for heaven, meaning 'the garden'

Allah used as the name of God in Islam

apostasy the abandonment of your religious or political beliefs

Arabic a classical language, spoken by around 150 million people throughout the Middle East and North Africa.

Archangel Jibril the angel who transmitted revelations to Muhammad

atheists people who do not believe in the existence of a God

awe a feeling of respect and wonder towards someone or something

ayats verses of the Qur'an

Barzakh the period of waiting between death and judgement in Islam

Black Stone sacred stone built into the outside wall of the Ka'bah in Makkah

capital punishment execution, the death penalty

closure for the victim's family the need to find answers and bring to criminal to justice

compassionate feeling of sympathy and concern for other people's suffering

crimes actions that are considered to be immoral and punishable by law

Dawud the prophet David, King of Israel

Day of Judgement Allah's final assessment of humanity at the end of the world

deterrent something that discourages someone from doing something

Dhul-hijjah twelfth and final month in the Islamic calendar

divinely ordained to be made a holy leader, chosen by God

du'a a personal prayer of the heart, often said alongside the set prayers of Salah

fitrah the natural instinct to know the difference between good and evil

Five Pillars of Islam five duties that are expected of every Muslim: faith, prayer, charity, fasting and pilgrimage to Makkah

forgiveness the action of forgiving someone for their actions

free will the idea that human beings are free to make their own choices

greater jihad personal struggle to follow the teachings of Islam and resist evil

hadd the most serious crimes in Islam, including theft and adultery

Hadith a holy book containing the sayings and actions of the Prophet Muhammad

hafiz/hafizah someone who has learned the Qur'an by heart

Hajj pilgrimage to Makkah

Harb al-Maqadis Holy war; the belief that Muslims may fight to defend their faith, but must not start the war

Hagar the mother of Ishmael and wife of Ibrahim

Hijrah the migration from Makkah to Madinah

humanists people who believe that their spiritual and emotional needs can be satisfied without following a religion

human rights basic rights and freedoms that are believed to belong to every person

ibadah obedience and devotion to Allah

ihram a holy state in which Muslims carry out the required rituals to complete Hajj or Umrah

Isa the prophet Jesus

Isma'il Ibrahim's first son

islamophobia dislike or fear of Muslims

Jahannam hell

jihad to struggle or strive for Allah. See 'lesser jihad' and 'greater jihad'

jinn elemental spirits

khalifah a respresentative and steward of Allah on earth

Kitab al-Iman the Islamic name for *The Book of Faith*

Iblis one of the jinn who chose to forever tempt humans to sin; also known as the devil, Shaytan or Satan

Id-ul-fitr religious holiday which marks the end of Ramadan; also known as 'Eid-al-fatr'

lesser jihad holy war or the struggle to defend Islam

low self-esteem having a low value of and confidence in oneself

lunar calendar an Islamic calendar which determines sacred months

Makkah the Arabic name for Mecca. Islam's holiest city, located in Saudi Arabia

Mina a neighbourhood of Mecca

mihrab an alcove in the qiblah wall, indicating the direction of Makkah

minaret the tower from which the call to prayer is given

monotheistic a belief that there is only one God

moral evil wrongful actions done by humans which cause suffering

Mount Arafat sacred mount where Muslims believe Prophet Muhammed gave his final sermon

muezzin the person who does the calls to prayer

Muharram the first month of the Islamic calendar

Musa the prophet Moses

natural evil things which cause suffering but have nothing to do with humans, usually as a result of a natural disaster, such as an earthquake

nisab the minimum amount of wealth a Muslim must earn before they need to pay Zakah

niyyah intention of attending Hajj

Nubuwwah the Islamic term for prophethood

Nuh the prophet Noah

omniscient the belief that Allah knows everything that has happened and everything that is going to happen

pacifism the belief that fighting, violence and war can never be justified

parliament the highest government legislature

passive resistance non-violent opposition to something

peace freedom from war and the fear of violence

pluralistic the positive belief in different types of people and cultures belonging to one society

predestination Muslim's believe that Allah is omniscient and knows the fate of every being

prevention of re-offending taking preventative measures to reduce the chance of someone re-offending, such as helping the offender to find a job

Prophet Ibrahim Abraham, the 'father' of Jews and Arabs, and 'friend of God'

Prophet Muhammad the prophet chosen by Allah to deliver his message

prophets messengers from Allah; there are 25 prophets mentioned in the Qur'an

qiblah the wall at the front of the mosque which Muslims face when praying. It is fixed as the direction of the Kaaba in Mecca

Qur'an the central sacred text of Islam, believed to be a revelation from Allah

Ramadan the ninth month of the Islamic calendar, in which all Muslims must fast

rakahs the sequence of movements in ritual prayer

rasuls prophets who were messengers that conveyed the message of Allah in holy books or scripture

reconciliation the act of causing people or groups to be on friendly terms again after a disagreement

repentance to feel regret or remorse for one's actions

restorative justice justice which focuses on rehabilitation of offenders through reconciliation with the victim and the wider community

resurrection returning to life, rising from death

retribution punishment for doing something wrong

revelation the Divine announcement of information, revealed by Allah to a prophet

Risalah the communication channel between Allah and humanity

sadaqah giving more to charity than just Zakah

Sahifah of Ibrahim an early scripture revealed to Ibrahim

Salah ritual prayer five times daily

Sawm fasting from sunrise to sunset

Shahadah declaration of faith, the first pillar of Islam

Shari'ah law legal framework of Islamic law

Shi'as Muslims who believe that Prophet Muhammad designated Ali ibn Abi Talib as his successor

situation ethics the doctrine of flexibility in applying moral laws depending on the situation

social justice belief that all humans are entitled to the same rights and privileges

subhah string of prayer beads

suffering bearing of emotional or physical pain

Sufism a mystical Islamic belief in which Muslim's seek to find the truth through direct and personal experience of Allah

Sunnis Muslim's who follow the orthodox way and believe that Prophet Muhammad's first successor was Abu Bakr

supernatural an event or thing that is unexplainable by natural law

Tawaf circling Ka'bah seven times on Hajj

Tawhid the Islamic name for the oneness of God

Tawrah the Jewish holy book

tazir punishment for crimes that are not as serious as had, decided by a judge

Ten Obligatory Acts the ten duties of Shi'a Islam

terrorism the use of extreme violence, often against civilians, to achieve political aims

ummah the worldwide Muslim community, the nation of Islam

upbringing the way in which a child is treated and educated throughout their childhood

weapon of mass destruction (WMD) a nuclear, biological or chemical weapon capable of causing death and destruction on a massive scale

Zabur the scripture revealed to King David

Zakah giving away one-fortieth of your savings for Allah's service